IN
VISIBLE
WATERS

IN VISIBLE WATERS

◆

JOHN BAILEY

Illustrated by Chris Turnbull

THE CROWOOD PRESS

Published by
The Crowood Press
Crowood House
Ramsbury
Marlborough
Wiltshire
SN8 2HE

British Library Cataloguing in Publication Data

Bailey, John
In visible waters.
1. Fishing—Great Britain
I. Title
799.1'2   SH605

ISBN 0–946284–80–6

Typeset by Inforum Ltd, Portsmouth
Printed in Hungary

Contents

For B.B.B.

Preface

There have been classic books this century and I am not so immodest that I expect to emulate them. Yet I do hope this will prove to be a new type of work and that it will inspire other similar but better attempts to master the concept in the future.

I have no desire to produce another factual A–Z volume on how to catch fish, nor a record of big fish captures.

What I am setting out to do is to study the fish itself. The fish in its environment, how it reacts to the seasons, to pressures, to lights, temperatures and foods. This is my theme. There will be no illustrations of the fish out of the water – this is the account of the coarse fish in its natural state.

Coarse Fishing is not just a 'hobby' or a 'pastime'. It is an art. From four years of age, coarse fishing has been a deep force in my life, not in a wild irrational sense but in a deep profound way.

Recently, I had dinner with a friend, a Vicar, a man I greatly admire. Christianity is the mainspring of his life. In it he finds beauty, purpose, mystery, inspiration and intellectual involvement. Fishing has fulfilled these roles for me.

The idea of writing the book came to me when I realized that, at certain times in my angling life, I had almost lived with a species. During these episodes all my angling time, thought and research becomes directed towards the knowing and mastering of a particular fish or shoal of fish. For a few days, weeks or months, I have felt so totally in tune with the fish and the location that my awareness has developed considerably. It is these intense periods that this book will set out to describe.

In the later 1970s, I met a man living in the eighteenth century gatehouse of an elegant time lost Norfolk Estate. It was an autumn morning when I first visited him, with mist on the meadows and hung on the avenues of trees down the park. In the small windowed gloom of his room, he showed me the most miraculous drawings of fish – drawings that put into tangible form the visions, dreams and observations of coarse fish that had filled my mind for over twenty-five years. We talked most of the day, both there in front of the fire and walking round the pools on the estate and we found we shared the same views and our experiences interlocked together. Dimly formed beliefs came together and grew.

Over the years we have fished and talked together and now I feel ready to write a book that I have lived with a long time. Chris' illustrations are a vital part of what I have to say: they put into the visual form what words alone can never hope to convey.

The observations that I have recorded in the book are accurate as far as my knowledge extends. Where gaps have existed I have gone to talk to acknowledged experts and some of the conversations I have had with these people have been fascinating. Chris Turnbull himself is an expert on tench and during his conversation with Martyn Page, I realized that here were two men very much in tune with the species and the environment and who had both thought very deeply about the evidence they had seen over the years. John Nunn is another of these thinking anglers who has helped me in several of the chapters, and is, I suppose, my longest time fishing partner. Vic Bellars knows more about perch than any other living angler, and tried his best to tell me a small part of his knowledge over an excellent dinner with his wife, Lindy.

To all these men, fishing is a very complex sport indeed and to them there is a lot more in life than putting a fish on the bank. The attraction is very much a knowledge of the fish themselves. It is greater because no man can ever know all there is to know about even one species, let alone all the freshwater fish that swim. Fish behaviour is a maze of eccentricity and variation. What Chris and I have seen and describe in one or two waters might well differ from your own experience. Please do not dismiss us for that: the water type, the fish stocks, the food levels, the fishing pressure – any or all of these things can have a massive effect and alter totally how fish live their lives.

Since we have met, we have caught both roach and rudd over 3lb, pike and carp over 25lb, perch of over 2lb, tench over 8lb, dace over 1lb, chub just short of 6lb, barbel over 11lb and crucian carp to nearly 3lb. I mention these facts simply to substantiate what we produce in the book, especially as very rarely again will there be any reference to any of our captures.

The actual production of the book has not been easy. While I had always realized that a book does not simply, magically appear, I had not clearly foreseen the problems that could emerge. Chris had at least as large a share of the problems.

To capture that sense, that feeling of water was difficult. When you or I look into a pond, we do not consciously see the water at all: we are just looking for things within it. Chris had to find a way of giving the awareness of a water film without letting it dominate the pictures, or detract from the fish we would want to look at.

Living a lifetime looking through the water, he had to imagine to some extent how our evidence from above the surface actually works below. And remember, he was working often in a multi-dimensional field. There was not merely the arrangement of the subject matter to think about, but the added problems of surface tension, surface light glare, refraction and water reflection. Given this mass of cluttering detail, his brush had to work in the same role as do our minds – sifting through the unnecessary and the distracting to concentrate on the important. Possibly the best example of this art is the painting of the crucian carp nosing through the lily pads. I have seen crucians look at me in this way a hundred times, and the representation is perfect, if perfection is possible.

We have all seen a carp roll in front of us at dawn, perhaps just a Mark IV's length away, have felt tremendously excited and have locked away the memory somewhere in our minds. No photograph can capture that instant water shattering happening: we remember it as we want to remember it, not necessarily as it actually happens.

Chris has seen carp roll before him too, but being very analytical he has never been convinced of what he saw in reality. When it came to draw the event, he realized that we all see in a carp roll what we want to see. It is a glimpse only and then gone. We expect the splashing droplets of water to be bright and dazzling, which they might be after sunrise when there is light to catch and reflect, but in the mists of early dawn, what colour are they then? It took Chris perhaps eight hours to catch the feel of that big mirror leaping in the half light.

His attention to detail has fascinated me. Fish scale patterns are hugely time consuming and yet he has sometimes discarded a day's almost microscopic work for being 'not quite right'. One evening I found him rooting in a nearby graveyard: he was at work on the rudd crashing into the falling autumn leaves – and he wanted to be sure that he had captured the reds and bronzes perfectly.

My problem has been to interpret the evidence fish have given me. For example, most anglers will agree that baby tench spend the vast majority of their formative period shrouded in the lake's thickest weed beds, but are they there for food, or for protection from their enemies, or to shield themselves from the harshness of bright daylight. The answer could be one or none of my answers. Or all three.

Neither Chris nor I would ever deny that we enjoy feeling a bend in our rods, seeing the float go away or putting the net under a beautiful big fish. But that is not the major part of what makes us fishermen: that is a love for the fish themselves and a desire to know more about their strange idiosyncratic lives.

John Bailey.
Itteringham.
1984.

Introduction

Sometime during the warm July night, a big seatrout stirred
in Tremadoc Bay and hurried with the tide alongside Shell
Island and over the shallow sands towards the fresh waters of
the River Antro. By dawn, the fish had made a couple of
miles and lay resting in the deep pool slightly upstream of the
bridge in Llanbedr village. The starlit sky above it paled to
the colour of mackerel and then softened to mother of pearl
and quite suddenly the sun rose to turn it into daytime blue.

The rapid Welsh river reflected light off every pebble,
stone and ripple and disguised the great fish well. He would
not feed, nor move; he simply lay current cradled waiting for
the night once more. Traffic to Harlech town grew and many
passers-by stopped to look at the river, but the trout lay low
and unnoticed. On the hotel wall sat a four year old boy.
Nothing else to do. Holiday time, parents still asleep. Watch
dragonflies. Skim stones. Look into the pool. Sometimes the
shadows there turned into fish and sometimes the fish
jumped like silver rockets. So, on the whole, it was an
exciting place to be.

One shape troubled the boy. It was the colour of a stone,
though shaped more like a post. It was the thickest end that
faced the flow and at the other there was a slight movement,
a trembling, like a flag lifting in the wind, as though muscles
were curling around the current. The boy moved his head as
if to see through the surface mirror better; held his hand to
his eyes to dim the sun's glare; moved position repeatedly to
get a better angle. He scanned the bottom inch by inch and
still could not make it out. He half closed his eyelids, hoping
for a sensation or a feeling of what the shape was. His eyes
were quite used to the water's lights, but he was still unsure.

He was called for lunch, went reluctantly and came back quickly. The sun was burning on the stones of the wall and even his brown legs became tinged with redness, but his dogged face peered on untroubled under a sun hat. The thought occurred to him to throw stones at the shape but, without being quite sure why, he discounted the solution as somehow beneath him, beneath the beauty and the mystery of the whole situation. Afternoons drag on towards tea time: the sun sank and the river became clouded in midges bringing the small trout to the rise. The depths of the pool again fell into the shadows and the shape hazed and disappeared, so he took a last fix on it and left.

Once the stars had returned, the fish began to move around the pool and as the moon rose, so it began once more upstream. But the summer had been dry and the river was low. Bleached rocks glimmered silver all around and the water was just a trickle between them, so try as it might, the seatrout could only get fifty yards or less to another of the hotel garden pools where it lay again.

At sun up, the boy ran to the wall and, head weaving like a cobra, searched the lie. It was deserted. It had been a fish. A great fish. And now the hunt for him was once more on. By lunch he had found him, the huge length and breadth, the same glints of silver, the quivering membranes of flesh at the tail. Now that he knew he was a fish he wondered how he could ever have doubted him. In this shallow water, he could see his eyes, his gill covers moving and the soft furling of his fins.

Once more he stayed with the fish until the shadows crept from the hills and the air began to cool and he was called away. He went to his room and to sleep, thinking of the fish and the morning and wondering if he would need to find him over again. But sometime, late on in the night, he was woken wide by shouting downstairs in the hotel and he made his way down the landing towards the staircase to the public rooms.

The seatrout lay there. He was quite recognizable by his size alone. He filled the silver tray. His captor celebrated in the hotel bar but the fish no longer seemed beautiful or mysterious. Any man could hold him and gawp at him. The wild was tamed and was of no interest to me anymore. I turned away and, to this day, I have never seen the need to kill a fish that is more fascinating alive than dead.

I · Mill House Barbel

There is not a fisherman anywhere that has not wanted to live with water in his garden. The idea of being able to fish, or watch fish, or feed fish without needing to travel is irresistible. Just being able to study an area of water, in all its seasons and moods, under blue skies and under stormy ones seems good to me. So when in 1978 an old mill house came onto the Norfolk property market, and when I shook hands on a deal, I had realized the proverbial dream of an angler. For the next three years we lived by water, and though we never wanted to, we could quite literally have fished through the window of our drawing room.

From the seventeenth century, the house had been used by an unbroken line of millers as a habitation, an office and even as an additional store place. In 1921, a fire broke out in the mill alongside and though the house was saved, the mill building was gutted and the towering walls have since been reduced to safety level. The water wheels, the machinery – everything was dismantled and removed, but the three sluice gates have remained, directing the river on down the valley.

Outside the house, are two mill pools and beneath them runs perhaps a mile of some of the most productive chub and barbel water in England. It was this, of course, that was the attraction of the place for me, and during my time there hardly a day passed when I was not walking, fishing or just watching the river. It was a living companion. Never before had I realized the constantly changing face of nature as I suddenly became aware of the effect of rain, droughts, frosts and snows in a much more intimate way. Not one day is ever just like its predecessor in the journey of a river.

Even to take a random yard of the water could be exciting

[5]

The Old Millhouse

– most of all rummaging along the bottom, finding pieces of old ginger beer bottles and the crests of long extinct breweries. Once I found the stem of a clay pipe – with a tiny lamprey encased inside it. Under every stone or brick or cracked old pantile there was likely to be a bullhead, or a loach or a crayfish to winkle out.

From time to time a kingfisher lived in the derelict building and in the year of the freeze when the shoals of fry and minnows lived under the ice, we fed him sprats on a regular basis outside the river door. In the spring, runs of elvers swam the river, stitching like carpets of needles through the sluices and, come autumn nights when there was little moon, it was damp on the ground with perhaps a storm in the North Sea, the mature eels would return past again, now silver in colour, ready to spawn, seeking the ocean to mate and die.

The trees along the bank attracted the squirrels and one, the last red, used to plant his nuts in ones, twos and threes all over the lawn and forget completely where they were. In the spring I mowed over a hundred mushroom sized trees.

Anglers always fished the mill pools, whatever the weather, but in those long summer evenings they would arrive from all points of the city and the bridges would bristle with rods all hung round with tobacco smoke to keep off the midges. There was continual angling talk of the mysteries of the pools or unwitnessed stories of 'biggies' had out; there were occasional shouts, the quickening rises of the chub and dace as evening approached and by the last light, the swallows gave the remains of the fly hatch over to the old mill's bats.

[7]

When all had gone, the pools quietened down enough to hear the owls in the copse downstream and you could watch the centipedes of city street lights to the south throw an orange glow into the night sky.

Very often, both day and night, we would be called out to witness, weigh and photograph catches. More and more the kitchen with its Edwardian range became a centre for huddling, talking fishermen. The coffee bills rose hand in hand with the mountain of ideas and stories of roach, or pike, or the occasional grayling, but generally of chub and that mightiest of river fish, the barbel.

My first sight of a barbel came two years before all this, on a bright late summer afternoon when I could see very clearly into all the nooks of the river. I all but stumbled over him, hard in to my bank and I was mesmerized. He was one of the big ones – into double figures without a doubt – and a big barbel really does look his weight. I suppose I watched him for a couple of minutes: he was obviously quite aware of me, because within seconds he became agitated, moved and went upstream lowering deeper and deeper into the water until I saw him no more.

Two minutes is quite long enough to effect a transformation: Paul on the road to Damascus and all that, but without claiming a miracle, the power, the determination, the shape, the size, the colouring of that fish, the massiveness of his bow wave against the current, all made me barbel crazed. Above all things, I wanted to hold one and look at it my total fill. This is so often the case: there is no element of gloating now or of pride or of hoped for fame. The delight is in the mystery of a big fish – the perfection of a living being that very few are ever privileged to witness up close. As I write, two weeks ago Chris Turnbull and I went perch fishing: Chris has never caught a big perch and as ill luck would have it, I caught the big fish of the day. But I do not think that Chris minded for one single moment. His joy in holding that fish, looking at its scale, its mouth, its fins, its colours, was obvious. This is what I wanted to experience with my barbel when I bade the furniture van farewell in September 1978.

So, for one summer, 1979, I devoted my life to the barbel; dawns, days, dusks, nights and whatever other hour God might send I was on that mile of river. For five or six months I got close to knowing next to everything that moved on it, be it a chub or a dace shoal, a weed clump or a barbel group. Right from the sluices by my window to the deeper sluggish water nearer to the city I watched and moved in on my prey.

The river helped me in every way: it ran clear and clean. In most swims, the bottom was visible for fifteen hours a day in June and only very occasionally did a summer storm slow my observations down.

As an angler, I was successful. By October, I had caught twenty-two different barbel, out of a river population of no more than probably forty or fifty mature fish. My last fish was my biggest one and I felt that it was therefore time to call a halt. There is no pleasure in re-catching the same fish and I felt that I knew the species as they behaved at that time. We even sold the house, to get away to something different and new.

Martyn Page has remained in close contact with the river and as angling pressure has mounted he has been able to witness the changing patterns of the barbel: certainly in four years those fish have adapted to some human induced problems and their behaviour has altered in several important ways. Most obviously, the way the bigger fish inhabit and use certain swims has been affected.

In 1979, I saw the barbel spawn. A dead elm overhung the spot so that I could climb 30ft above the beds to get excellent sightings. They used a fan of gravel swept by two flows of water. The depth was 1–3ft and the whole area not much more than that of a tennis court and laced by abundant streamer weed.

There was little difference between the courtship of barbel and say, chub or tench, except to say that the groups of fish involved were usually smaller and that between four and eight fish taking part was normal. Like carp, they chased together in small groups, frequently coming together in explosions on the surface. It imprinted that unique barbel swimming movement forever on my brain, that cross between the trout's dynamic thrust and the eel's body length wriggle, that coming down the line and through the rods, gives a fisherman an unmistakable sensation.

[9]

The gravel became the focal point of the river's entire life for a while. Minnows, dace and all the small fish species closed in – presumably to get at the eggs – and they were followed by chub, the occasional perch and several jack pike. The heron spent the bulk of his time in the area as did kingfishers, a grebe and a growing colony of rats and crows after the left overs.

When all was over and the activity died away, the barbel remained in the area all of that summer. Certainly, it was their spawning ground, but I got the impression that the features of the place suited them perfectly at other times and that if left alone, they were happy to remain. Within a stones throw there were two good overhung runs, thick with trailing branches and heavy spent weed rafts that the fish used extensively for shelter during the daylight hours and whenever they needed sanctuary. That summer, there were always barbel under the rafts: on dull days or early in the morning the fish would spill out from underneath them all over the river but in brighter conditions all you would see were noses, a drifting tail or a straying 'baby' elbowed out of the clubhouse and looking for a way back in.

The river bed in the area was kept clear of silt by the still lively flow of water from the nearby mill and the gravel always looked clean and healthy with rich beds of weed rippling over it. There was a wide variation of depths, the place was isolated from roadside disturbance and I thought that it must represent the perfect swim that fish would never leave for long.

Perhaps so in my day when the pressure on it was slight but now the situation has changed. Martyn tells the tale of Bo – one of the most beautiful big barbel in the stretch – who always used the spawning area but who now has been forced out and uses all the river. In a short period of time she has been seen here in deep swims, slow swims, shallow and fast swims. If untroubled a barbel will lie for weeks, but in modern angling worlds they develop a nomadic existence.

What he says ties in well with the Old Girl down on the Hampshire Avon – an 11lb fish, an old and dear friend recently told me about. She, in one year, was taken in four different swims, spread over nearly a mile, with a major weir

having been crossed once going downstream and negotiated again by the fish returning upstream.

These two fish illustrate several points. There are not many big barbel in this country I suspect, and certainly many of them are known by name. I do not doubt that unknown fish do exist but in some prime rivers the same big ones keep coming out. I think the names themselves also show a certain affection that barbel fishers have for their quarry and it certainly highlights the problems of the often caught fish debate. There is little doubt that the catching and re-catching of certain fish can do great harm. Pike, because of the indiscriminate use of large multi hooking systems, and because of the temerity of inexperienced anglers when faced by a phalanx of sharp teeth, suffer very badly and have a high catch to death rate. Small easily caught fish on popular waters often suffer from torn lips, missing scales and split fins because of poor handling and being kept in keepnets.

Fortunately, in the case of both Old Girl and Bo and with several other specific big barbel, little obvious harm has been done to either their condition or their weight. Anglers who

[11]

catch such magnificent fish are invariably dedicated to the care of their fish. A played out barbel, for example, must be held upright, facing the current whilst it recovers and can move off under its own power. Both Martyn and I have let barbel go too soon only to see them turn belly up in mid-river: neither of us have hesitated to strip off and dive in to recover and save them. I suspect we would not be alone in doing this.

So, if we do not do harm to a fish by re-catching it, it is very probable that Bo and the Old Girl, having been caught, probably move swim and lie low for some time. When they do come back on to the feed, they appear to do so with a gusto that replaces lost energy and food reserves. Certainly, one 11lb fish that I caught and returned within a minute, I observed feeding very heavily some fifty yards away the next day, the trauma of the experience seemingly relatively short-lived.

Probably then, the major effect of such re-catching results in the nervousness and nomadic urge of the fish being increased. A travelling barbel generally uses the upper layers of the river to move in. It is obviously easier for the barbel to swim nearer the surface where it encounters far fewer obstructions to its progress, from weed, snags, bottom contours, tree roots and the general debris that litters any river bed. Quite probably, the barbel uses this upper zone to form a greater awareness of what is going on above the surface and a better assessment of angling pressure. Over shallower water the bow wave of a big travelling barbel is impressive with frequent sightings of the tail and dorsal fins. They are

easily disturbed and will then either move very quickly up or downstream or, if over deep water, simply submerge into the weed growth.

Barbel often pack together in certain famous swims and to this extent, they do therefore shoal; but it is a loose shoaling tendency and more important is the common desire of the fish to use the best swim available. If that swim for any reason loses its attraction, then the barbel abandon it in ones and twos until the area is all but deserted. They do not though, move at once in a pack as roach or dace would do and in most cases the bigger fish sense the falling appeal of the swim and evacuate it first. One dawn, for example, I found at least twenty-five barbel feeding hard on the gravel run outside a major tree raft. The fish ranged from 3–12lb and they were quite content living and feeding as a compact shoal. After two hours of watching the fish (I made no attempt to catch any) a water worker arrived to close down a sluice; within minutes the flow of water over that particular swim was greatly reduced whilst the opening of a second sluice had increased the current elsewhere.

Three big fish were the first to leave, travelling in the surface zone forty yards downstream until they found a flow more to their liking. Over the course of the morning all bar two of the barbel followed their example, leaving in ones, twos and threes until over twenty fish were re-positioned in the new swim. Again they were a shoal, but they had not reacted with typical shoal mentality.

This behaviour pattern is also demonstrated in the species reaction to an introduced food supply large enough to lead to pre-occupation. All species become pre-occupied to a greater or lesser degree and it is dangerous to say that a barbel is any

more susceptible than a trout to a caenis hatch or than a tench to a daphnia explosion. However, the reaction of barbel to hemp is a sight to see. This is not a phenomenon on my river alone: Gerry records it on the Stour and Avon and to see master angler Ron Lees at work with hemp and barbel on the Severn is unforgettable.

In simple terms, the taste and smell of hemp has a great effect on barbel, drawing them from some distance into the swim and generally inducing a feeding spell that can be hectic. I have stood behind Ron Lees as he arrives at a swim on the Severn and almost the first thing that he will do is to put in a pint of hemp seed. Then he tackles up, whilst the seed begins to work its magic and long streams of small bubbles illustrate the arrival of the fish into the swim, all heavily on the feed. Ron's first few trots down, often with a maggot or a caster bait, can result in a fish, and even whilst playing it he will continue to heap the seed into the swim to keep the others occupied and head down.

On my river below the Mill House, I have frequently started with an empty expanse of gravel, though I have known barbel to be present in the vicinity. As the hemp goes in and settles and the juices trickle away in the current, whiskered noses begin to appear from out of reed beds or from under overhangs and the first few fish arrive over the seed. Other fish drift up almost unnoticed – in ones and twos until the gravel run is a mass of feeding fish.

Barbel begin to roll as the pre-occupation sets in. They come out of the water and arrow back in at speed, going down to hit the bottom. Here the second part of the movement is performed when the fish on impact with the gravel turns onto its side and rubs a yard along with its belly flashing in a dull ivory gleam. The entire action takes a second or less but the images of the barbel breaking surface and the deep flash remains longer in the mind. Martyn describes the roll of a barbel as a joyous occasion, sheer exuberance, children let out of school or at a party: at a party is probably the nearest as they want to seek out the very last tit bits. The barbel have picked out the bulk of the tiny seeds but they know that grains have been swept under stones and into crevices in the gravel and they gouge at the bottom, desperate to dislodge them. Sweetcorn, maggots, casters and other seeds and peas will interest barbel, but none seem to have the galvanizing appeal of hemp.

Barbel, especially hemp induced fish, will feed from dawn, at any time during the day to dusk and into the night. Without any doubt though, under normal circumstances the favoured feeding spell takes place at last light and even into darkness. All barbel rivers are likely to come on at this time: it is a universally known fact from the Stour to the Severn and I assume that barbel, like roach, eels and bream rely on a reducing light factor to trigger them into feeding activity, and their suspicions of baits is much reduced. On the Avon, Gerry was used to seeing grains of food lying untouched all day on silkweed covered gravel, but by first light the food would have disappeared and the white gravel showed up in a maze of lines through the silt where the barbel had hoovered up both food and weed in their night's patrol.

2 · Bream

Over and over in this book, I have been made aware that though you might know something about fish behaviour, it is quite another thing to be able to explain it. Bream are a case in point and they come near to being my favourite species because of their ability to do the bizarre and inexplicable. I might feel that I recognize many of their characteristic habits, but I can never really say that I truly know the fish.

As an example, one very cold winter night I went into Gunton Park, Norfolk, as I had planned to fish there the next day and I wanted to check that the place was not frozen over. I drove to the iron bridge that spans the channel from the Sawmill Pond to the unfishable Great Water and looked out over the landscape. There was a three-quarter moon, a clear sky and a fresh to strong south westerly that despite the wind frost, was able to keep the centre of the water open.

The moon's reflection beamed off the broken water and quite deliberately, framed in the silver light, a big bream rolled, fifty yards from me in only two or three feet of water. Only the one fish moved, quick as a bat's shadow against the street light, and friends have said I saw a coot, a duck or perhaps a log bobbing up, dislodged by the wind. But I know the sight of a rolling bream and that was it, something I would not before have believed on such a freezing night. It could not have been feeding, but nor should it have been travelling through the fast icing shallows. There was just no sense to it that I have ever been able to see.

BREAM BROAD

My first encounters with really big fish came the summer I

[16]

found Bream Broad. A farmer's permission, a fox path track
through developing alder carr and softening ground, a boat
house of rotted Edwardian punts and there was Umma
Gumma, blue, bailable and just fit to row. The dyke gave
way to the full broad and when I got fifty yards in, I simply
sat there. I had never seen anything as beautiful in my life.
Around twenty acres, a jewel set in a wilderness of woodland
and though a wind was bending the tops of the birches and
the oaks, the water itself lay like an eternal mirror. Reed
fringes had encroached on the softer banks, soldiering out
along their promonteries, creating caves and bays. There
were lily beds and dragonflies above them and whether
Umma Gumma drifted over two feet or ten was no matter –
every detail of the lake's bed was distinct and clear. Yes, just
to sit there was quite something; to know that nothing visible
had changed at all over the centuries and that, as far as I cared,
the world could simply leave when it wanted to with me and
Umma Gumma on Bream Broad for ever.

But I had the rumour of bream to check out and the humid
day was crackling into a close-by storm so I stirred and poled

gently to the far end of the lake. What breeze there was blew down the water and I stood up to act as a human sail. I wore polaroids. I had uncased binoculars around my neck and as I glided the length of the Broad I scanned all points in front of me. There were swan mussels, the occasional eel eyes blinking out of a head swaying above the silt, occasional shoals of small rudd and two bolting bronze tench, but there was not a bream on the whole body of the water.

I made three drifts, each one covering a different lane, and still the place looked bream barren. The storm was now really about and the wind had picked up, so I hit the weed fringe at the end of my last journey and decided to sit it out in some kind of harbour. The water had shallowed out to no more than 18in and the reeds were in virtual command and hard to pole through in my search for dry land. Ten yards into them I broke into a small bay, right at the extremity of the water, which from the air could have looked like a bobble on a night cap. The water there was welling slightly – there was no immediate sign of bream – but the whole bay looked on the move and I knew instinctively that I had found them. I slid over the mudweights, hit the deck and little by little lifted my face over the tattered clinkerboard. In front, were five bream drifting in water barely deep enough to cover their backs: there were their scales, the rays of their fins, their gills slowly on the move and I could have touched them all that miracle day in June.

Bream from a poor water are a miserable species, losing all depth and thickness of body. Their colour goes and they are shaded in greys and whites until they look spectre fish, not true flesh and blood, not true bronze bream. These fish were bull shouldered, stocky backed, bronzed nearly to black, yet with a head that was still small and neat. More and more fish pushed by the bows of Umma G., all the same classic shape. Last of all came six bream that I really believed could make a nonsense of the record as it stood in those days.

After the storm, I rowed back into the creek a wet and chastened man, drove off for provisions and tackle and for the next six weeks I hardly ever left the place. My partner was J.J., who joined me most nights to fish, whilst each day I spent afloat with the bream. What I learned, I do still believe

[18]

was important, and the fishing one night was climactic.

Together we fished long and hard off a landing stage at the deep end of the Broad. Night after night we put the sessions in and we caught good bream, a seven and a half pounder especially sticks in my mind. Those very big fish we never did contact though, until a night into August.

There was a big moon, and I did not rate our chances with both that clear bright water and the cold night that hovered on the brink of a frost. We fished though, as we always do, and at midnight, J.J.'s indicator crept up like a slowly rising star. He waited until I thought my nerves would break and then lashed the rod through the sky past his shoulder. Eleven feet of hollow glass bent round almost double. What was on the end did not spurt off like a foul hooked, middle weight fish, but hung heavy and unrelenting in the water. J.J. and I looked at each other and nodded. We both knew that this was the fish we had spent our nights awake for. I often wish I had a photograph of J.J.'s compact, black silhouette on the boards, the rapier bend of the rod against the silvered sky and the dark smudges of the bats flickering around his line, wings sometimes catching . . . and I can hear his soft curses now, almost ten years later.

After a long while, he moved the fish that had fought and slogged for the silt, and it came in towards us. I sank the net and looked across the waterline and, as I did, a back came out that made me gasp and J.J.'s face tightened. But then, damn it, the bream began to kite, faster and faster, drawing across us, to the left, towards the rushes alongside the landing stage and it got there with a smash and a crash, like hogs hitting kale.

Everything had gone wrong: the bream was fast, Umma G. was down the other end of the Broad, locked up, so we could not get to the fish and it had to come to us. The wise J. Judge tried all he knew, and despite the cold night, I saw beads of sweat on him. I asked for the rod, to try an old carp fisher's trick I knew, and such was the trust between us, J.J. passed the butt into my hands. All the way down the rod, I could feel the bream's head shaking and I strained to keep it free: a beautiful, beautiful feeling, I felt the fish come free, swimming again. I gave the rod back to J.J., a slam of

[19]

pressure pulled it down as the fish spurted back into the open Broad – and then nothing. It had shed the hook.

We sat down. We had a coffee. J.J. rolled a cigarette. Not a word passed for a while: it was for him to comment first. We had another coffee, steaming away into the loveliness of a cold Broadland dawn, when J.J. spoke: 'Well,' he said, 'it makes all the effort worthwhile.' At that moment I thought the man was mad, though now I wonder. After all, the drama has remained and even for me, grown in the years since. None of those big bream was ever caught. They lived and by now they have died big, amazing and inviolate fish. Only, I can at least say that I know something about them.

Since those days, there has been a theory that bream shoals follow particular patrol routes, rather like sheep paths, around a lake. The idea first appeared concerning the fish of the Cheshire and Shropshire meres and I am sure that this is how the bream of these far larger waters do travel, but here on Bream Broad, I would use the concept only loosely. The bream did not follow any exact tracks around the lake at particular times, but the twenty-four hour cycle did indeed witness a number of deliberate responses.

In the vaguest terms, at night, most of the bream, no, I cannot say that, a lot of the bream would move sometime from the shallows to the deep end of the Broad. I have got to stress the word *sometime* too, because from one night to the next they could arrive in deep water at any moment from dusk to dawn. Nor did I sense that there was any special route that they followed: one night they rolled close in, the next far out and the third just as likely in between. It was not a case of setting a watch by their movements, or of fishing to a particular line. They were just not so clear cut.

Similarly, in the daytime the bream would be in the shallower end of the Broad nearly always, but it was impossible to forecast where until they were actually sighted. Neither time nor weather helped any deductions and it seemed they went by chance. Indeed, the bream often behaved in what appeared to be a totally irrational way. Small groups of up to six fish often milled around the shallows in a quite haphazard fashion, moving quickly and frequently changing direction. It is possible that the nearness of Umma G. produced this

Chris Turnbull 83.

effect and threw them out of their normal rhythm but at
other times they accepted the boat without any show of fear
at all. This type of behaviour might be thought typical of a
pre-spawning ritual when groups of males chase their mates,
but it did continue throughout the summer without spawning taking place.

As the groups of bream travelled, fish rolled frequently
and their slab sides caught the light and bounced it back in a
shield like gleam. As they went down again they hit the silt
bed and it billowed in a mud cloud behind them. The bream
never went back in to investigate for disturbed nymphs and
worms so presumably the action was not a feeding manoeuvre. Perhaps the fish were cleaning themselves after
spawning or were trying to shake off parasites, though the
fish I did catch were quite clean of any lice or leeches.

On hotter days, the bream acted more expectedly, drifting
in large bodies around the reed bays and hanging quite still in
the most sheltered areas of water for minutes on end before
casually moving off once more. Very much like carp, the
bream obviously enjoyed sunlight and warmth, drifting with

their backs clear of the surface, flexing their dorsals, not a care on their minds.

The next year I was in Umma G., when the bream were spawning on the Broad. The focal point was a column of rushes that had broken away from the main body and had become an isolated pioneer surrounded entirely by 4ft of water. Between thirty and forty fish were active around the roots, frequently coming to the surface to thrash in a ball together, only ending as individuals exploded away in furious bow-waves. Silt clouds smoked up all around, staining the water and the whole swim was riddled with eels, obviously after the eggs that the desperate bream were pumping out.

A number of the bream died during spawning, coming up sometimes bloodied around the flanks, and drifting into the coves behind. Three very large fish appeared in this way and I buried them further back into the marsh to keep the jays from their eyes and the rats off them. Over the following days, the eels in the area grew in numbers and fed heavily all the daylight hours and, later in the summer, despite long searches, I found no stocks of bream fry.

Nor did I ever see trace of the black bream of the Broad. They were supposedly seen by one who knows the place well: coal black fish with fins of a vivid scarlet. He swore to their existence and though I looked and looked, and fished and fished, I never clapped an eye on them myself. I wish that I had. I can imagine them as fabulously beautiful, as the ultimate secret of this marvellous water.

BURE FEVER

Some time ago a book called *Bream Fever* was published. It was one of the first specialist coarse angling books and deserved to succeed for that, and for a chapter on Norfolk's River Bure. Those years back, the words had a magical effect: the unspoilt countryside of the Upper Bure Valley, the clarity of the water and the shyness of the fleeting shoals of bream attracted me greatly and marked the Bure bream down as a target for the future.

From my house now, from the table where I write, you go

east, alongside a stand of young conifers to the hill's crest, cross the field and look for a minute at the rabbits playing in the great crater in the ground that is the Devil's Dish. Now you are dropping downhill and soon come into a belt of marshland and then to the Bure itself. So far upstream, the only fish are the native brown trout, but go downstream to the Mill and in the pool there, the roach begin. Two mills further down and the river begins to widen and deepen and you are into bream country.

Looking back on the summer I first searched the Bure, it seems to have been all a summer should be, very warm dust in the lanes, and a freckling of poppies alongside the corn fields. The water was as clear as its reputation, frequently deep, with good gravel and chalk runs, rich in water cabbages. The towpath was overgrown in most places, and you had to beat through to the next bend, to reach the next copse, to get to where you felt no man had fished in a decade perhaps. Bream were not easy to find, though it was no hardship looking.

At Oxnead stands a church and a hall and you drive past both to get to the river. Now, fishing is private, but then you parked by the poplar wood and walked downstream half a mile to the open fields and the sand bed where children swam on hot days. Two meadows on and you came upon the thin wood where the river bottlenecked and ran deep. The reeds grew out thickly and I steadied myself amongst them and looked in on a swim full of bream. The sun was already slanting down and I could not see everything I wanted to, but I had found Bure bream at last and I walked back upstream impatient for the morning to come.

I was back tackled up and settled in before dawn. The sky paled quickly and the water started to glow with mists. From my feet almost and for thirty yards downstream bream rolled steadily and heavily, showing very dark against the surface. It still was not light enough to see a float and I had to watch a bobbin that held against the easy current. I was soon into a fish, a good one that hugged the bottom and got the cabbages above its back, but he came up at last. A seven pounder with a neat head and short thick body that was coloured a dark chocolate brown.

I had others, then the swim went quiet and then dead. The bream had gone. I picked them up again a bend further down where the King's Beck enters the main river and they had chosen to lie in its mouth. I stopped fishing and watched them the rest of the morning. One very large fish was with them, but very restless and soon it left, heading upstream. When I too started back to Oxnead I came upon him again, still moving quickly and by now into the wood; his back was pushing a vee of water behind it and he was easy to follow. I put a worm before him and he went down after it, caught a loose end and swam with that in his mouth until he felt the pressure of the tackle and then he spat it out and merged into the bottom weed.

I saw that big fish very often after that. Unlike the major shoal, which stayed on at the Beck, he remained highly mobile, showing anywhere between Oxnead and Buxton, two miles further downstream. Since, I have come to think he was very unusual for a river bream, which will generally hole up in a swim until disturbance becomes too great and they are forced out. Certainly fish will live out their entire lives in a mill pool or in a deep enough slack or eddy. Perhaps the fish was diseased in some way, or had been caught and returned, but he certainly looked tense and continually agitated.

3 · The Carps

If ever a fisherman, a coarse fisherman, thinks of summer, he thinks of carp lakes. He remembers short, still nights and dawns come early when the bees are in the honeysuckle before five. He sees in his mind mists and rising moons and setting suns and leather backs basking in milk warm lakes. Over again, he hears pigeons, woodpeckers, kingfishers, jays, the explosive splash of a carp on the water and perhaps his reel giving line. Close his eyes and think himself on a carp pool, and he smells wet nets and the scent of a bait flavouring on his hands.

If ever a fisherman, a coarse fisherman, dreams, he dreams of willows and carp lakes, of ones he has fished, ones he has heard tell of, and the ones he will only meet in Heaven. There are waters imaged in every carper's mind, fabled, famous places like Beechmere, Redmire, Mapperley, Ashlea, Swancoote Pool and Woldale, where he would be just happy to sit and stare and never even need to fish.

I love all fish and there is not one species that is not very special to me for some memory I have of it, but I do realize that the carps are different. They are larger, they live longer, they have individuality: they are not common fish and to generalize about them is impossible. To talk here about the carp I have witnessed in one water alone is possible, but it would betray the species as a whole, which is nearer human than fish.

The most beloved carp writer, B.B., once wrote a book in which he described his 'gallery of carp waters' and I do not think that I could use a better approach here, if I am to do them anything like justice.

I have been putting in a lot of time on the River lately, but today there was bad weather on the way and it came early, long before lunch-time closing. So I ordered another and sat back before the fire.

'Mind if I join you,' asked a big, bearded man in well worn Barbour and boots. 'Not up the river today – don't look surprised, I have been fishing in the wood all week and I've seen you as I come and go.'

Here was a conversation that spelled interest. A shadowy fellow fisherman to get to know seemed at that moment a deal more appealing than a force sixer and heavy rain for four hours. So I replied that I could not take the River for another day and I was staying put. Could Tilly get him a drink . . .

I believe we soon felt that we saw things much alike – he told me about a badger on his land and we discussed the return of sparrowhawks to the county. We talked about roach a lot, and pike and bream, but whenever fishermen get together at some time carp will be mentioned. We both knew the same waters, had fished the same swims, possibly caught the same fish and had been following in each others footsteps for years, but yet had never met. Strange, I suppose, but then we are both the type of angler who likes to fish alone and can shy off if there is as much as a car parked by our favourite waters.

I asked him about his biggest fish. 'I won't answer that one,' he said 'but I will talk about my best! My best carp was a 7lb wildie from Gibbet Pond.' I at once agreed that a 7lb wildie is indeed a marvellous fish, and is the equal of any other common or mirror four times that size, and to take it from Gibbet Pond, I said, was nothing short of miraculous.

It is a pond of an acre or less, dammed half way up a hill to make an old duck shoot. A century of silt has shallowed the place off to no more than a foot of water and it is always possible to see the two shoals of fish swimming from end to end, or stopping off to feed on the way. There are only wildies in the Pond, put in years back, now as hardy as old eels and not much deeper in shape. In winter the water freezes solid for weeks and in a hot summer it is as though the

[26]

plug is pulled on the place, but those fish live on through it
all.

I learnt there that the drinking, wallowing cattle attract the
carp to them and that they swim feeding in the silt round the
cows very hooves. My new friend explained that was exactly
how he fishes the place, to wade around a small area for
fifteen minutes and the wildies would flock in. Such is the
way he caught the seven pounder . . . and he once saw a nine
pounder come out. Now this I really was on the point of
disbelieving when I thought myself of the case of Lockhart's
Pond, no bigger in size or depth, that I had fished for years
and had a hundred and more wildies out of.

Indeed, I had caught my first ever wildie from Lockharts, a
good four pounder, that at the time I thought had jumped
out of Heaven itself. Like all real Wildies it was long, slim,
not thin, with a cream white belly and strong as brass scales –
I had dashed round to Lockhart's door to ask if I could fish
the pond for ever! As far as he was concerned, he told me, I
could, and that one summer before a ten pounder had come
out. I forgave him this story easily for after all, every country

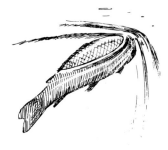

pond has to have its legend and this obviously was the Pool of the Myth of the Ten Pound Wildie.

In fact, I worked a lot on Lockhart's farm and got to fish the pond more and more and never once did catch a carp of more than 6lb. In later years the pond grew to be overstocked and the size of the carp declined with a three pounder becoming an uncommonly good one, so I fished there less and less. True I heard the report of an 11lb wildie in the years I was away, but I discounted it as the Myth. But then, last summer, a man I would gladly trust with my life went down to Lockhart's and he told me that he caught a wild carp just one ounce under 12lb and so, for me, the Myth is true. The carp was as long as a crocodile with horny old scales that made it look as though it had been alive for ever, but, you see, it existed.

I told my friend this tale and he nodded. He knew the pond and had heard tell of the fish. For a while we made plans to capture him ourselves, but in the end we decided against it. After all he was the wisest, cleverest fish ever to have lived in a puddle twenty years and only be caught three times. He was a legend and he should remain so. If he is ever to be caught again, we decided, then it should be by a young boy or an old man, or by somebody who would be amazed and call the fish a miracle, and not by a calculating expert who would simply then cross another challenge off his life's list.

I told my friend about the two big wildies in the Marl Pit behind the White Hart and those in Docking Pond, and he told me about the ones in the Green Pool, right by the village stores. By the time we had finished we decided there was a wildie or two in nearly every pond, pit and puddle we knew – and in all probability, it is to Saham Mere that this county owes its wild carp.

If ever you want to watch wild carp, go to this place. It is the ancestral home of all wild carp.

They thrive everywhere, but at Saham they are irrepressible. It teems with them. The water is pea-green from their continual silt riddling and on a still morning the whole surface lifts with their bubbles. Thick reed frond stretches out from the margins, with the water only inches deep over foul smelling mud and tangled with fallen tree branches and in this jungle, the carp live more like amphibians than fish. They will swim with all their back exposed, they will take food that is right out of the water and they will slide over on to their sides to get in to the shallowest dips. There is nowhere I know where the complete eccentricity of the fish is shown better.

One summer I camped on the little island there with a stack of provisions and bait and by the end of the week nearly every fish in the lake had marked the place down and was there for a feed up. I was catching them on whatever I cared to use: bacon fat and beans, bits of sausage, or almost anything at all. They were so hungry. Yet they fought well and looked fit. It was as though they just could not bear to miss out.

Tilly had been making it quite plain for a while that we should leave. Dusk was not far off to end this crabby winter day and as we stood at the door, the occasional patch of blue appeared in the skies. The wind had done its job. The heaviest of the rain was done. There could still be time for a roach or two after all . . .

OWLSMERE

Owlsmere was dug long, long ago. In a valley, it marked the divide between two parishes and it served a large working farm with water for all its purposes. Great care was put into keeping it a thriving pool: every few years, during the slack time that immediately preceeds the harvest, all of the farm men were put to mucking out the silt. The water was drained away and in the hot early August weather, they carried off the rich deposits in bucket and barrow and spread them over the cattle pasture. The farmer only called his men to a halt when they were so deep that, from the mere's bed, they could no longer see the chimneys of the house.

Even though the cattle drank the water and waded and basked there in warm days, the pool always remained clear for its spring fed waters ran like the purest ice. Water cress grew around the outfall, the alder trees bent over the dam wall and there was always a white owl resident in the barn that overlooked the whole scene.

The constant draining of the mere meant that fish had little chance to establish themselves. Sticklebacks always managed to find a puddle in the silt and to live on until the water flooded back in. So too did enough loach to keep their numbers healthy, but any bigger fish, bream or tench, were taken off to the table. Mucking out time always surprised some eels that had made their way from the river a mile up a feeder stream, through a disused moat and along the drainage ditch that wound through the wood to the sluice gate.

Sticklebacks and loach kept the kingfishers quite happy. They nested most years in the sand bank and only the hardest winters set them back. The eels always attracted the heron who divided his time between Owlsmere and other small waters that nevertheless had more fish in them. Frogs, toads, newts, a mass of beetles and bugs, swallows in the summer time and that was about it in Owlsmere in its prime.

But the place began to decline. The tenant the past half century could farm no more and the estate took back in his acres, leaving just the house, a couple of meadows, the barn and the water to his family. Neglect set in all around: the outbuildings to the barn collapsed and the weeds marched in triumph over the flowerbeds right up to the boundaries of the vegetable garden; the hedges grew wild and disordered; the track became pitted and impassable with mud by winter; the house itself suffered as the gutters dropped away and the window frames steadily rotted into worm eaten decay. But of all, it was Owlsmere that changed the swiftest.

No longer dredged, the silt from the fields settled and built up. The springs became buried and weaker and soon in the driest weather, they barely functioned at all. After not many years, the ducks and the two remaining geese could touch bottom almost everywhere and needed to swim only over a channel hard in by the dam. In winter, the first hard spell of frosts would freeze the mere all but solid. The reedmace began to close in and year by year lengthened its fingers over the pool. The outfall became choked, the stream no longer ran, the water cress died away in stagnancy and the eels turned away from the place. Soon nature took back what had been hers and Owlsmere then was again nothing more than a green marsh with standing water only after heavy rains.

The Mirror Carp

YELLOW
FLAG
IRIS

ROSE BAY
WILLOW
HERB.

DOG ROSE.

CREEPING BUTTERCUP.

One day a lorry arrived at the top of the track and a digger was unloaded and made its way down to the old water course. It was March, very wet in the valley and even on its great caterpillar tracks the machine skidded and nearly floundered. Since the mere had filled in the drainage of the entire area had been poor, but the driver got to the dam and began to work. As his bucket removed bog, water instantly appeared in the hole just as though Owlsmere were not dead but merely sleeping. It was like a man digging in porridge, hard unpleasant work, but little by little, water began to spread up the valley.

The machine worked well into the spring and when it left the waters of Owlsmere were in area as large and in depth greater than during its original years. Mud and silt lay everywhere along with banks of spoil so that it looked as if the very guts had been torn out of the valley. Summer greened the scars though with grass pushing through from April onwards. Trees were planted in late March along the western bank, white willows, goat willows, guelder rose, dogwood, common alder and field maples. The rich, moist soil helped them to thrive in the following hot summer and a careful check was kept on the wire cages and the spiral guards to keep out the rabbits. Only one night a roaming herd of red deer camped in the valley and chewed off the tender shoots of some twenty trees, some of which, afterwards, were always to grow a little crooked, as a result. Some nut trees seeded themselves from the ancient hundred acre wood on the north and east and the growth of all was rapid.

Only a few white and yellow water lilies were introduced, in cages, on the shallower banks, as already the roots of the previous plants like the water crowfoot and the arrowhead were beginning to reappear. Even around the banks little planting was necessary as the water mint, purple loosestrife, soft rush, creeping buttercup and willowherb all began to recover and spread over the moist mud deposits. A few wild dog roses were dug in here and there and a couple of iris as well. Several colonies of common reeds remained from the past and they too filled in rapidly. At the revitalized outlet of the mere, where once more the fresh clear water ran across the gravel, rocks and stones to join the stream, the water cress again appeared with its tiny white petals opening like stars by the second Maytime. By this second spring, the pool looked very nearly beautiful once more.

Another lorry arrived and struggled down the track that fell off into the woodland and made its way over a quarter of a mile to where the roadway led across the mere. It stopped. It was bringing a consignment of carp. The fish were both mirrors and commons, about eighteen months old, but of such a fast growing strain that already they averaged around 2lb in weight. Particular fish stood out already as getting ahead of the rest. One deep backed common looked to be close on 3lb and a pale ivory scaled mirror could not have been much smaller. All had suffered slightly torn fins and lips from the journey, but they would recover well in the un-stocked, large lake and as they went into the crystal water they formed a huge shoal of twenty or more fish. It hurried around the shallows for some minutes, a single, fast moving body of carp, and then in streams of bubbles and silt, dis-appeared into the deep central gulley which remained to mark the course of the old stream. Not for a week did the shoal come out.

Watching the introduction of the carp, was the last tenant farmer. In Edwardian days he had been born there and he still lived in the house with his wife and mother. Between them they had been over two centuries at the farm and had never fallen out of patience with the place. He still worked the vegetable patch, loved to watch the rabbits on the stubble fields, the barn owl that worked its way down the water course to lose itself in the evening mists that rose off the lowlands. So, to watch the mere come back to life was a joy to him and made him feel that the farm was not yet done.

Just as the baby carp had gone down, so, when they re-emerged, they came as a shoal; rarely, if ever, that first summer, did they break away from each other, but rather travelled, fed and basked together. Perhaps, by the autumn, the shoal sometimes divided into two or three groups of seven to a dozen fish, but no one fish would yet swim alone.

There came a season of violent storms. For three weeks, nearly each day after noon the sky began to darken, the thunder approached from the south west. The carp came to

[33]

the surface in the sultry heavy atmosphere, swimming with their backs out of the water, sometimes gulping oxygen from the air itself. When the storm was very close, many began to jump, completely clearing the surface, whilst others bow-waved over the mere sending sticklebacks shearing before them and even putting up the mallards with their violence.

When they broke, the storms came short and sharp, often with up to half an inch of rain and a strong breeze. The water of the mere cooled rapidly as the skies let in fine blue evenings and long fiery sunsets. At that time the baby fish went down to feed on the silt beds raising foam, bubbles and stained water long after nightfall.

The final storm that year began to brew in the mid-morning. Hour upon hour the sky piled up heavy clouds, low lying all the way to the horizon, and flashes of blinding light licked across the landscape. The carp were beside themselves, dizzyingly active throughout the day, the shoal moving tight together, always travelling, using the whole surface of the mere.

When the rain eventually came, it fell for over two hours and was recorded at over an inch in the old farmer's glass. Streams dry for years rose and gushed into the mere until the water seeped over the banks and cascaded down the valley.

The old man saw that the dam wall was on the point of collapse and called for help. Emergency sluices were punched open and clay was heaped against the appearing cracks until the tide slowed, steadied and receded back once again.

OWLSMERE. SECOND SUMMER

By the second summer, when the fish were three years old, their growth was apparent. Each of them now was quite distinct to look at in the clear, blue green water. That largest common carp was looking more and more bull like, with shoulders that towered out of the water when he tore towards floating foods whilst his head remained small, well shaped and neat, almost out of proportion to the huge body he was quickly developing. The ivory mirror carp was still keeping up in size, but the colours of the flesh and scales were increasing in their brilliance until now the sheen was of a gleaming near white that showed the fish way off, even deep down in the gulley. Under a full sun both of these fish glowed quite flawless, the one golden the other more silver in bright light, the opaque silver of a full moon under light cirrus cloud.

All the carp were now fully settled and growing in size, in colour, in shape and in character. The shoal that had sub-divided now broke up further and fish in ones and twos were quite happy to explore all over the lake and feed and bask behind the islands, in the extreme shallows, or in the corners of the dam wall.

They came together to exploit very favourable food sources however. The farmer still kept his bullocks and after he had carted them bales of straw, and had closed down the chicken sheds for the night, he would on most still pleasant evenings take a bag of corn or maize down to the mere side and feed the fish. All the carp felt him come and gathered in the bay that he always chose, milling round and round, taking the grains as they hit the surface and as they slowly sank. A mouth full, each moved off to chew and swallow and then came into the area again and the cycle was repeated.

The very big common generally fed on the bottom. By the dying sunlight, he could just be seen tipping up into the mud and silt, burrowing through the layers, bubbling and heaving, taking in the mass of the sunken grains with anything else edible he could find. He levelled off the bottom to chew infrequently: he ate harder and longer than any of the other fish, even more than the ivory mirror. When the old man left the water and went back across the meadow, the rest of the fish dropped off the surface to compete with the big common. Their bubbling and chewing pushed lost grains further into the silt and they furrowed deeper and deeper to seek them out. The bay was coloured chocolate by the time the old man closed the farm house down, sharpened his knife on the old grooves cut in the red brick work around the back door, and bedded in for the night.

The fish were three years old and in the September a man came to the lake with a fishing rod. He moved very slowly around the waters edge, sliding in behind clumps of reeds and using the trees to break his shape. Sometimes he looked

intently into different bays through polaroid glasses and then he would scan the water further away with binoculars. Half a day he stalked the pool in this manner before he made his first cast and only five minutes after he landed the big common carp. Two hours passed and the ivory mirror fell to him.

Both fish were played gently but firmly and the barbless hook was taken out whilst the fish still lay in the folds of the net. Caring not to touch the carp, they were guided into a weighing net and the amazed angler saw how quickly they had grown. In one single year they had more than doubled in weight and he had to check his balance again. The mouth and fins of each carp were still flawless: the scales were still immaculate and within seconds of their capture, each fish powered back to that deep central channel for refuge.

The old man was watching and was awed by the size of the fish. 'Will you fish here often', he asked the man.

'Not again for many years', the angler replied, to the farmer's astonishment.

'Then why do you do it all? Why did you dig the mere out again, and plant the trees and get me to feed every night?'

The angler laughed and said nothing, but as he sat there on the dam listening to the stream fall away down the evening valley he did think that he might well have created what could one day be a legend.

THE WOOD PIGEON COMMON

Wood Pigeons is a large, old lake set completely in forest land, roughly crescent shaped, dotted with islands and bitten in by bays. Common rushes mark the water line, there are frequent flotillas of white lilies around all banks, but other weed life is usually absent however warm the summer. But the most unique characteristic of this beautiful lake is the purity of the water – not even after a storm or a gale or a flood is its remarkable clarity lost.

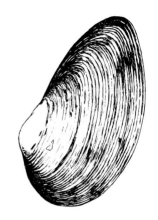

You can see a swan mussel drag itself at twenty five yards, a grebe catch a roach at six feet and an eel hole even deeper down but more than all this, out there you watch the shadow of a great fish. Even through field glasses the actual body is vague in the radiance of the sun lit water, and the slow moving reflection seems to be the only solid manifestation.

The image of this fish is moving out of range and you have to cross a headland to follow him. He is probably going into a bay on the windward shore so you get round there fast. You see nothing either with the eye or with the glasses, but a carper's senses built up through the years tells you he is in there, so you get down in the rushes, amongst the mud and the nettles and you wait.

The sun is at its highest, making life hot out of the breeze. There are dragonflies over the water and squirrels in the trees behind, but on the mire around you are wasps. A stench of marsh gas lies like a sickness; the glare off the water, the concentration of focusing through glasses all day have combined to give you a headache. The squat hunch you are in has brought on a cramp in your calf and a stiffness in the upper thigh. Your back hurts, perspiration runs in your water boots, there are flies on your forehead and down your shirt, but somewhere the fish is here. So you do not move. To see it will mean everything.

Again, at last, you see the shadow. It is edging down the bay towards you. No fish. Just that zeppelin shape of darkness over the lake bed and a shoal of roach fleeing before it. It stops barely five yards before you and dimly you see scales and slight vortices on the water. Forward again and now it drifts nearly to your nose. The huge Wood Pigeon Common is before you, quite perfect in every way. Its long, untorn, dusky purple fins are on the ripple and in the bull head the eyes move constantly, unscared but untrusting. The gills bellow rhythmically and the body sways slightly to the pectoral beat. The barrel vaulted sides bulge close enough to touch. He is girder ribbed and one day in death his carcass will lie like a hull on the lake bed.

You are seeing the fish in only eighteen inches of water – the scales of his back are pushed clear of the surface and the sun sparkles on them. They are a horny brown. He looks like a tortoise caught out in a shower. Even whilst you take in the hugeness of the fish your eye is aware of the Lilliput of the scene. There are alderfly larvae in the silt and stones, a beetle rows past and the fish's eye traces the course of a water boatman.

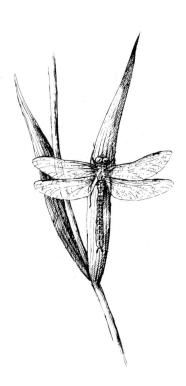

Over five years I have followed this fish and never have I been so close, so now, perversely, it stays with me all the afternoon. My body has gradually seized with cramps, pins and needles and flickers of old rheumatism until only my eyes and brain seem alive. After all the years of wanting the fish, could I now catch him? Now that we are pals could I want to feel him run, pressure on, steel in? Could I ever hold him, hot hands on cool body, and let the midges batten on to the gill covers where the taut nylon has chafed away the leather skin and brought out thin lines of blood? My biggest common carp lies there, but could I catch him for the fame, the photograph, the pride?

There is no real dilemma. I have no gear with me. He might not take a bait – he never has in the past. He would get to the fallen elms on the island and break me up. I am dreaming ever to think of the creature as mine for he is too mightily beautiful to belong to anything but the lake of his birth and his life.

He lies there, so vast, so unmoving as if he is always still, but he is capable of dynamite. I first saw him five years ago after long sessions on the lake when I had come to believe only small carp were in fact present. What caught my eye then was not a shadow, not a fin or a back, but a slow solemn bow-wave between two islands. I was quite sure it was a hunting grebe or cormorant, but the uneasy feeling grew that it might be a fish.

The Great Common Carp

The power bulge of water got in behind the near island. No bird re-appeared and in chest waders I forded the deep silt to the outcrop of trees. The land itself was too overgrown to make a path through and I paddled around the shoreline, pushing past the fallen thorns. Behind the island the water was sheltered and south facing and I waded blindly, the bright sun in my eyes. The bow-wave came for me fast and I caught the merest sight of the fleeing fish exploding back into the open water in a comet of bubbles.

Twenty yards away and the common came out of the water and I saw him clear for a second and knew him to be the monster of the Lake.

There are other carp in the Lake – about eighty all told – and there are times when they come together as a vast loose shoal. Most usually, this happens from early June when the commons begin to assemble around the weeded shallows where they spawn. They do not do this successfully every year, but they still flock there and chase and bask there until mid or late July when they increasingly break up and go their separate ways either individually or in groups of half a dozen fish.

The big common is always present at these times, though despite his enormous size, you often would not think so. He hangs just off from the main group, where the water shelves from two gradually down to eight or nine feet. For hours on end, even if you know he is there, all that you might be aware of is the occasional suspicion of a large shadow drifting on the shelf or a particularly large 'flat' on the water where he has turned just under the surface wind ripples.

Very occasionally, the big common comes onto the shallows with the other fish. He shows an almost endless repertoire of movement in what will perhaps only be a stay of a few minutes. He might swim very quickly, crisscrossing the area in a series of bow-waves, sometimes going down into the silt to bulldoze a smokescreen of mud and torn weed. He might cross the area in a series of water shattering jumps – and once I counted sixteen in the space of only a minute. Another time I witnessed him lift himself out of the water, seemingly on his pectorals, look about and sink back only to repeat the process again and again for several minutes. Frequently he swims on his side – not spawning – but swimming quickly through the weed beds, his vast belly gleaming a golden bronze.

Or he might simply hang in the water, moved only by the currents of the breeze – like he is doing this instant by me in the bay. I love the way he is flopped in the water, unbalanced, uncaring like a tired man in a warm bed who flakes back without effort. His fins barely move, he is simply washed over by the water and yet you know that the power can be flicked on in a second and the great tail could roar him back into open water. I have heard carpers say that such big, wallowing carp are ill or aged or dying: rather they know quite how to relax and enjoy themselves.

When, in full summer, the smaller fish leave the shallows, the big common nearly always departs as well. He is a traveller all right and will happily move a couple of miles in a day when the mood takes him. Most of the way down the eastern side of the lake runs a steep, rabbit holed cliff and from the heights, with binoculars, you can watch him over a hundred yards away, moving like a purple galleon. All the day, the weed wandering carp stays on the drift until night hides him up.

You would think that, given decent light, he could never escape from you, and yet days, even weeks pass when I do not see him. I sit on the cliff, with binoculars and food for twelve hours or more and I can never see a sign of him, only the smaller fish going past. I can search each of the lily beds, paddle around the islands, but he won't be there. Once I found him in the dark of an underground boathouse, but only once, and at other times I have almost again begun to think that he has died. But he always re-appears.

There are two grey squirrels now, fighting up and down the trunk of a pine tree, the claws scratching into the crevices of the bark, sending the cones falling into the dry undergrowth. I have been so still for so long that they are chasing right now into the tall grasses that meet the reed bed, enraged, chattering, furious with each other; they are almost on my boot, squealing with rage, and when they do see me, they hop back in shocked silence before melting up the tree once more.

The common is beginning to stir now, probably because the light is fading and the shadows are cooling just enough to tell him evening is on the way. You can sense that he is becoming more alert by the way the folds of fins are starting to stretch once more. His mouth begins to work more and his eyes are increasingly active, all as though he is stretching and yawning, suddenly bored.

His head sinks until he is on an even keel, then he turns and the water begins to lift above him. At first he drifts and the movement is slight, but as he leaves the bay, he picks up pace and the bow-wave surges in to the beyond. I can hardly move, and I limp off amazed with what I have seen.

CRUCIANS

The day had been very warm for October with constant sun once it had sucked the mists off the land and the water. There had been no breeze however slight, and the woods were like beaten copper. When it began to sink, the sun dropped quickly and there was one moment when it hung right on the turreting of the hall. At that instant, a flight of starlings appeared and wheeled around and around in the dazzling sky. They crisscrossed the lake, whooped in and out of the crenellated sky line, rose and dipped, turned broadside and flattened out again in a vast aerial manoeuvre. A thousand starlings, in perfect time to a tune that only they knew, dancing and waltzing the last of the daylight away. In a sweeping curtain, they draped over the lake and again as one,

settled into the gold drenched rushes to the east of me.

The sun had quite gone now and the pheasants called goodnight from all the roosts in the park. A bedtime in a gun man's estate before the season gets properly underway is deafening. Vollies of sound: breaking of branches; angry cocks disturbed; fights in the fallen leaves – something like a rural rush hour. It heartened me in a way – for the crucian fishing that day had started bad, got worse and ended in complete and utter hopelessness. So I left my rod and walked over to the lily bed, huge and ancient, nearly a quarter of an acre in extent, to take a last look at it for this crucian season.

It was dying back fast. The flowers had long since gone and now the great pads were withering and sinking until there was more water than green – no, not green, more olive turning to brown. Worse, the lily bed was unmoving: no stems twitching, no pads lifting, no princeling crucian carp turning this way or that to catch the sun, or to avoid a breeze, no dragonflies striking blue over the flowers and no shoals of fingerling roach remained any more. Nothing remained anymore to say what a place it had been in the happy summer months; I turned away back to my tackle.

Should I fish on into the dark? There might yet be a crucian somewhere in the lake still willing to be caught – but I doubted it. You know when the time is not right. They would wait and I could spend a long winter thinking about this species that is so essentially a part of the English summer scene.

The crucian is small for a carp, a little round odd ball of a fish with mellow yellow scales, cute mouthed, blunt tailed and tough as old leather. A pixie of a fish. (When I got indoors, I wondered why, vaguely, I used such a word to describe a fish. My dictionary definition of a pixie is 'a supposed supernatural being' and to be *pixie-led* is to 'be led astray' or to 'be bewildered'.) I used the word exactly right: this summer I have been 'pixie-led' by crucians to the limit of my understanding.

My rod was still out over my favourite swim. This is fourteen feet deep, or fifteen after any rain. Now, I can get these fish feeding on corn or maggots or mashed bread – feeding I am sure they are by the trails of high density fizz bubbles where there had been none before the groundbaiting. In the midst of this hyperactivity, the crucian splash happens. Often several crucians splashing at one time. This seems a totally unco-ordinated movement. It is noisy as though the fish does not know quite whether it is coming or going, as if it has got its timing wrong and is trying to turn back to start again. I have witnessed hundreds, perhaps thousands, of these appearances in the past and can only analyze them as a brisk sideways turn on the water surface with a kick of the stumpy tail fin to send them on their way again.

But, being pixie-led, I cannot possibly understand why crucians should expend such furious energy on what would seem to be a pointless manoeuvre. They obviously rise at high speed and are probably as quick going down again. In this very deep swim especially, I cannot see why they should waste valuable feeding time to travel five yards up and five yards down like a piscine yo-yo, simply to tell the world it is lunch-time. Ten yards of temperature, light and pressure change must be an Odyssey in the life of a creature only eleven inches long.

Martyn Page explained the roll of a barbel as a joyous occasion. Joyous may be too human an emotion ever to apply to a fish, but perhaps excitement is not, and is nearer the mark. My good German Shepherd, Paddington, gets excited, wildly so, at food times, and hops and skips and jumps at the mere sight of a tin opener. The cats react very similarly. The ducks and geese on my meadow get excited, flap their wings, fall on their beaks, trip in the mud when I simply walk to the grain shed. So, in a not very different way, do I suspect that these big lake crucians are reacting to my offerings.

As I take my tackle down, an owl is going through the wood and by his calls I realize he is following the main drive that leads almost to the village. Old saucer eyes, I think, picking up every beam of light the rising moon can throw out. The lily bed begins to shine under the growing silver intensity – but no, it is the reverse actually. The lily bed is in fact dark and it is the water that is gleaming around it. How many evenings have I packed away like this, with the crucians still sucking and kissing at the pads, quite audible this fifty yards away.

Then, of course, crucians slurp at everything: the pads, the fallen rhododendron leaves, sunken branches, things they never have a hope of eating, or even the desire to. Watching them close, I see that they are skimming off the algae, the microscopic food film of daphnia sized items that even a pixie hook would be too large for! Perhaps their curiosity plays a part as well. It is their way to investigate everything in their world.

Fifteen years ago, for four years, I had a crucian in a tank by my bed. He long outlived everything else put in with him – dace, roach and perch all died – and in the end I put him back in the same pond he had come from. He lived totally unperturbed by everything, except by an eel that I once foolishly put in with him. He was chased and bitten for a miserable day before I removed the repulsive wriggler.

Every bit of food put in the tank the crucian sucked at, blew in and blew out, over and over, until it was sufficiently softened and crushed to take back to the throat teeth. Maggots, bits of worm, bread and sweetcorn were all treated in this way, but the most remarkable demonstration of the habit came when I put a jam jar of tadpoles into the tank with him. He, and they, went quite demented. He sucked them in, rolled them around his mouth and blew them out again, sending them cartwheeling away into the far corner. He spent hours at it, sampling every tadpole in the place, hunting them out from under stones, or from amongst the weed, but I do not believe that he ever swallowed one. They were all eaten eventually, by the perch but not by the crucian.

I know it can be a doubtful exercise to draw conclusions from captive fish, but in this case, I feel the lesson is fair and I can say that so many of my bites have come to nothing this summer. I was sucked and blown and I rarely had a chance of striking. A bait that is interesting enough to stimulate curiosity in the first place and which is already very soft in the second place, would, I know, prove to be the ideal crucian bait.

This curiosity crucians share with all the members of the carp family, but they take it to investigative extremes. Saham Toney is a village in Norfolk with a mere ancient enough to be described in Domesday. The water is roughly round, about ten acres I suppose, and I had some marvellous days there with the wild carp and the crucians, though it is private fishing there now, I believe. By accident, I discovered that if the bottom silt were disturbed and then the landing net drawn through the cloud, very often crucians would be caught. On most visits I tried this unusual way of crucian fishing and very, very often I was successful. Curiosity in the stirred debris was great enough to draw fish right up under the landing stages; I cannot think of another species that would react in such a way.

But then, compared with the other bigger carps, crucians lead very circumscribed lives. They are quite happy in the tiniest of ponds and in bigger waters they do not travel widely. I have repeatedly caught the same fish from the same swim over a period of several seasons, and with no other evidence I feel that they are not great travellers and are not as aware of their environment as the much more nomadic big carps. Physically, crucians are not shaped for 'the road'. They are stocky, not streamlined. A hooked fish bears this out. The fight has none of the long determined runs made by a mirror or a common carp; the crucian seems to have no thought of getting out of the swim, only to bore in short sharp bursts into the snaggy areas it knows so well. There can be a thrilling battle, but it would have probably covered no more than a yard, or at the most a rod's length.

The fishing van is waiting on the keeper's track. There is heavy condensation on the roof and the windscreen with a whiff of frost in the clear starlit skies, so perhaps it is no surprise the fish failed to feed. There are two long dead grey squirrels nailed to an oak tree near me. Between two posts stretches the keeper's line; crows, jays and two foxes hanging all like sad washing. Nothing must disturb the holiness of the pheasant wood. It is the pheasant that keeps the wood intact and saves it from becoming absorbed into the agricultural part of the estate and, if that were to happen, the lake would lie exposed to Northerlies and Westerlies. Then the crucians would never feed as late into the year as they now do. Nor would I like to see more chemicals getting into the water than already do so now. There have been two fish kills in recent years. The countryside is no longer a safe place for pheasant, fox or fish.

The wood looks best in the dawn, when a sheen of dew paints it translucent and the rising sun sparkles off diamond fields of droplets. Crucians feed best at dawn. There is no doubt of that. Evening and just into darkness can be good, but that period around sunrise is unbeatable. Then they are

[47]

great little bubblers, sending them up in trails that mark their route. It is not unusual to see ten or a dozen separate wandering lines of bubbles around the swim, drawing crazy patterns, sometimes coming together over the hot spot.

Tench, carp and crucians are the great bubblers of the fish world and I am still unsure how the effect is produced. The silt cloud so often created by the searching carp is relatively easy to understand, but bubbling is by far a more complex action. The crucian in my tank never produced a single bubble that I ever saw, though I tried introducing all sorts of beds into the tank – silt, gravel, sand, fine mud, they all failed.

A common explanation is that gas from the bottom sediment enters the fish's mouth, and escapes through the gill rakers, but by then broken up to give the usual effect of tiny pin prick air bubbles. However, I am not happy with this idea. George Sharman in *Carp and the Carp Angler* examines the question better than any other writer and his explanation is that waste matter and the bottom gas interact in the intestine and that the bubbling effect is air leaving the vent, not the gills.

Certainly only fish bottom feeding produce bubbles and the air is not bottom gas pure and simple which comes up in large, irregular bursts. So somehow the air is being produced by, or at least channelled through, the fish.

We know that clouds of bubbles prove that crucians are in the swim and that they are feeding, but yet I have never caught more than an isolated fish at these times. I sit, tense, excited and invariably leave flat and let down. I doubt if I am even getting bites. I begin to suspect that the crucians are in fact burrowing under my bait to get at natural foods in the silt layer. But why does my groundbait trigger off these bubbling spells, if it is not itself being eaten? Damn them: we do not know the truth: I only write what ought to be the truth.

4 · *Chub*

THE RIVER DANE, CHESHIRE, 1962

It had been a raw day, somewhere around Christmas time. First it had blown wet: soaking cold rain driven across the heavy meadows of the Cheshire plain. When the wind veered northerly, rain gave gradually away to sleet and eventually, by the late afternoon, to snow. Long, long before then, I had found fishing impossible. A thin overcoat, jeans and short boots could not keep out wet and cold like this. My gear was canal tackle, too light for a river beginning to rise and colour and my concentration had gone.

In the mid-afternoon, I found cover down one of the deep cut banks where I dug myself into the rich soil. By me, an angler was still fishing, trotting lumps of flake far bigger than the snowflakes, down a twenty yard run and into a tight bend. His red float was easily visible on the river, bowing to obstructions, nodding as the line was mended, jostling with the rougher, boiling current on the edge of the slack. He was working hard, casting, trotting, retrieving, in very little light; and at the last of it, he got one.

When I saw that chub, for an instant, on the white ground, something happened to me. Its size, its colour, its shape – I took them all in and my heart quite melted at the sight. I walked back to the farmyard as the moon rose behind a veil of soft falling snow flakes. I waited for the family car, sheltering amongst the cattle sheds where it was warm with breath and dung, and I decided then and there that one day I would get out of the city for good, become a countryman, and catch a lot of chub.

Chubbing at dawn

FRANCE 1967

Like Cheshire, this is the story of just one day, now a haze of memories. Some small chub lying under a willow tree; a white waterfall; a wide, Normandy river flowing through corn meadows; a perch I took sometime around lunch on a small silver spoon; after, on a hot afternoon, I walked along the bank, on no real path but on more of a sheep track which took me to a great lake.

I am sure now that it must have been an oxbow. It was very clear. Clearer than crystal. No, the water was clear to the point of being invisible. The surface was freckled with water lilies. A heron waded at the far end of the pool and kingfishers worked over the water continuously. On the far side of the lake rose up a wooded cliff: by me, there was a wide sand bank to the wide slow river. The lake was not deep and here and there small, single tree islands sat up out of the water. I had no camera then, and I was never a drawing man, so I committed it firmly to memory, so firmly there is no mistake about the place.

The sun moved a handsbreadth through the sky whilst I sat there on the sand. I was aware of more birds, of how every leaf of every plant and reed and water weed supported life, and I was aware of a group of chub passing the time beneath a bed of lilies. Grey fish. Lips of creamy white that came up sometimes to suck in a struggling summer insect. Tiny fish were always on the move before them and so, taken all in all, I knew the giants to be chub.

In the long grasses, I caught a cricket and I hooked it up and cast it to lie in the film of water around the pads. The chub all came close. The insect struggled gamely and the rings of the water radiated out from it over the fish. They became agitated and they began to look for the victim bound and waiting. They found the cricket and the first chub rose and swirled away. Then, like the sun rising from the sea, the second mouth swallowed him down and my line tightened after him. I lost the chub . . . and the cricket and the hook, but I had got nearer my aim.

In later years I tried very hard to find that lake once more. I bought maps, I toured the tackle shops in that department, I asked men on other river banks and I even went to find the man who had taken me there as a boy, but though I found his home, the family had moved on to another part of France. I looked for three days, but this time I was on business and could not stay on in the town further. So, as you can see, I have never been back.

MILL HOUSE ON THE RIVER WENSUM, NORFOLK, 1978

Now, at last, the moon seemed to be at my feet. I was out of any city and I could catch chub as I wanted. They lived all around the house in the river there, that ran by the window, and in the two pools that lay just outside the mill walls. I began to see them much more realistically and as my knowledge of them grew, their remote, mysterious aura vanished. Now I saw the chub for what it is: a fish of infinite possibilities.

A chub will feed at night, and in the day. He will feed on the surface, in midwater and off the bottom. Neither flood nor drought will sicken him and put him off the feed. His food can be virtually anything edible from the common to the uncommon to the bizarre. He can be clever and shy one day, and equally dull headed and stupid the next. One day he will eat anything all the time, but the day after nothing will tempt him. Some chub travel and others will live in one swim for years, just as some chub shoal and others will live largely solitary lives. A hooked chub might turn out to be an angry fighter scrapping every inch to the net, or a defeatist that turns up its fins after only half a rush. On the bank, some chub look fat, golden and powerful whilst others are an ashen grey with battlefield scale loosened bleeding sides. At the Mill House, I saw them all and when I had done catching them, I took simply to watching them and they became friends of a sort.

THE CHUB YEAR

Towards the end of February and into March, many of the chub that had spent their winter in deeper water downstream began to migrate upwards towards the Mill House, or more exactly, towards the streamy gravel runs beneath the two pools. Big fish, unseen for months, by the end of March had re-appeared in this steady spring long procession of the chubs, but first it was the smaller fish that returned in great numbers. Water that had held few fish right through January now became dark with chub until by May the quick water was heaving with them.

When their spawning began, the thrashing of a thousand or more fish was clearly audible from inside the house itself, even above the roar of the sluicegates. The tension of these stream held fish was electric: a single fish breaking the surface would set a whole group in motion and a frenzied reaction would set in until the whole river erupted into a maelstrom of arched backs and quivering fins. If the weather warmed more and more fish pushed from below and then for a day, or even two, the spawning could seem almost continuous. The chub showed little fear in these periods and you could watch day long, seeing old friends come up, recognised by scale wounds or fin malformation, and you would wonder how much they had grown and feel very pleased to see them still alive.

Spawning finished, the chub fed hard: lean, hungry fish always searching the current, investigating any possibility of food. I remember one year Manchester United were playing Arsenal in the Cup Final and as I watched the screen with my left eye, my right was on a 3lb chub in the river outside. Now a Manchester United Cup Final is the occasion for much beer and excitement and twenty minutes into the game I rather felt the chub should participate in the event. The refrigerator held an exact pound of cheddar cheese.

Half-time saw a great deal of the cheese gone and by the time United were beaten by the odd goal in the last minute the chub was wiping its lips over the last morsel. Gloomy though I was, life must go on, and I continued to feed the fish bread and it ate six thick slices before it could take no more and sank into the weed. A pound of cheese, the good part of a loaf and that 3lb chub must have weighed near 4½lb before it said no more. A remarkable case of post-spawning gluttony, but I can think now of others that nearly matched it.

The need of the chub to feed had sad repercussions. Chub, like a lot of species, stay around their spawning areas for a while and at the Mill, they like the well oxygenated water and the gravel and so were still present in numbers come the start of the fishing season. June 16th invariably saw very heavy angling pressure and a great number of the fish were very easily caught. Three weeks or so after spawning and they were still ill-conditioned fish; they were often caught by inexperienced fishermen, allowed to thrash on the dry bank or even the roadway, and then kept captive in overcrowded keepnets for overlong periods. There is no doubt that season after season, the chub suffered greatly. Many lost scales and sometimes they were scarred for life: many had lips torn or twisted which developed sores and ulcers: most had split fins that took well into the summer to heal.

So it was that the first two weeks of the season left me despondent. Nature had driven the chub into this sickening vulnerability which the unthinking anglers were all too happy to exploit. There were times that I was glad not to have refound that childhood French paradise so that I could always remember those fabulous fish there, untouched and unharmed. This annual slaughter of the chubs at times made me despair about the morality of some anglers. It bore the resemblance of bullying and I could do nothing to stop it.

The chub, themselves, of course, found the solution soon. Firstly, the big masses of fish broke up and quickly they departed downstream in small groups. Here they found more sheltered swims in far less accessible water where the fishing pressure on them dwindled considerably. Secondly, the majority of the chub very quickly wised up to men, baits and tackle. By the mid summer most of the chub had become once again very hard fish to catch.

How I loved those summer chub and to go after them just before dawn when the world was still asleep, when mists lay over the meadows and when even the horses and cattle were tired and uncurious. My tracks in the field dew, a heron starting away from the dyke and the smell of damp loose-strife on the banks were daily things to me then and I miss them now I have moved away.

The chub had been feeding, probably all night, and were

still away from their daytime lairs and a bait on any of the open gravel bars could well be taken. That is where they made for at dusk, hunting those nocturnal creatures that make a chub's life worthwhile – elvers, lampreys, loach, bullheads and what crayfish that still remained in the river by those days.

Below the mist, in the grey water were even greyer shapes. As the dawn light strengthened, it bounced sometimes off a broadside of scales and gave a dull bronzed gleam and you knew the chub were still there turning, twisting, feeding. Total masters of their environment they were always willing to come up to the surface to investigate any bits of luck. Crust they loved, and were wary of.

They would kiss at it, dunk it, nose it, splash at it, hit it with a caudal fin or two, and only actually eat it as disintegration set in. Those drunken, ambling morning crane flies they loved especially, and the sequence was always the same: the unmistakeable, sad looking daddy on its long legs trying to lift off the water; an intent eye an inch below it; and then the nose, the splashy rise and a boil where fly and fish had a second before been. I often wondered . . . did he really want those spindly good for nothing legs, or did he spit them out, deep down over the gravel, for the gudgeon to play with later in the morning?

A trout is a very fine fish. Nowadays I fish for them as much as any of the coarse fish species, but I accept that they cannot ever compete with chub for opportunism, sharpness. They are not nearly as 'quick on their feet'. My northern mates would have said that they lack what chub have in plenty, that unspellable word *nouse*. See what I mean. A trout hangs in midwater, eating nymphs or passing beetles and bugs. Or, he comes to the top, after a while, when it has become very obvious that a fly hatch is under way. Perhaps, if several minnows swim past him, under his very nose, he might decide to attack the seventh or eighth and might even catch it.

A chub, though, will eat a beetle then, a moth now, a stickleback next and after that wherever a victim appears within five yards of him, he will have it. It is only an angler who can change this total awareness by ladling in pints of

un-natural food which will gradually drug the chub into only accepting the bait and into ignoring passing, juicy, alternative courses.

Some fish shoaled, though in their own distinctive way. For instance, a roach or bream shoal tends to stick together through thick or thin until the last remaining survivor, perhaps after a couple of decades, dies to become a floating carcass at the lock gates. The chub, however, seemed to be more flexible, and formed small interchangeable groups. Some fish would leave, others join up until some shoals became like come-as-you-please parties. Exceptions of course existed. Three fish outside the house windows always stuck together, certainly over the four years I had knowledge of them. Only winter floods ever hid them up, and once the water cleared, then there they were together as usual.

And of course, certain fish always seemed to live in certain swims, sometimes even ignoring the spawning scramble. They never travelled as did the group chub. One fish in particular was always at home. In 1902, upstream of the house lawns, a thatched boat house had been constructed. By my day, the place was pretty tumbledown and, in fact, in 1980, it fell down, but a slack of water still remained at its mouth. All my time at the house, a chub lived in that hole and, during daylight hours at least, it never seemed to move, though probably at night it went roaming. I caught the fish the first summer it was in the place and it weighed 2lb 8oz. It never moved for twelve months and then it weighed 3lb 3oz. Nearly exactly a year later it had grown to 3lb 14oz and by the fourth year, when I reckon it was 7 or 8 years old, it looked around 4½lb, though I left it alone.

Come October and November, many of the best chub began to drift downstream away from the shallower faster water. A lot of them moved a mile or more to where the river widened and deepened and there they struck their winter quarters. The chub did not do this alone for the roach and the stretch's few bream tended to follow them. I suspected that the migration had to do with the increased flow of the river and the fact that the bigger fish were looking for slacker areas where they would have to work less hard.

Certainly, around the Mill the river did flood easily and often. On one occasion, as the water receded, I walked over the sodden meadows and in the knee deep water several small chub fled off in front of me as though I were a type of huge heron. There was no way I could catch them and return them to the main river, but I never found them stranded when the flood finally drained, so perhaps they did make their way back.

5 · Dace

I first became fascinated with the Falls stretch over fourteen years ago. The tales were that it had been producing some huge dace, some even over a pound and I started to visit the place. I have fished there every year since, have had dace of massive size and begin to feel I know the beat very well. Above all, I have begun to have a great regard for the piece of river which over a three-quarter mile stretch provides shoals of fish with all they ever need in their lives. This, then, is a guide to this remarkable stretch of water.

The Pool itself, which heads the beat, is not large and has over the years silted up considerably, giving few depths over 6–7ft where 10–12ft was the norm. This has had obvious effects on the dace stocks. Now they tend merely to use the pool periodically, whereas once there were fish continually in residence. This tendency has increased as the flow has declined in summer months and the growth of the nearby village has led to more children using the Pool as a swimming and play area. Throughout the year now, the place is occasionally employed by canoe groups which contribute greatly to the unsettled nature of the modern Pool. So, what was once the prime dace swim in the river is really no more, and apart from a few small fish, it is necessary to look downstream for their new haunts.

The tail of the pool is very shallow now and even in winter it is generally possible to walk over the stones from bank to bank where at the end of the 1960s there would be 3 or 4ft of water. The lessening depth has hit the entire population of the run badly: crayfish, loach, bullheads and gudgeon have moved out completely leaving only a few minnows and very small dace. Because of excessive field drainage up the valley

during the 1970s, the river is becoming increasingly like a northern spate river, quick to rise and fast to run off. The force and fluctuations of the water effect these shallow gravels especially adversely and, like the Falls Pool, another one time great area is in decline.

Beneath the tail, the main river is joined by a tributary from an overflow pool, and the confluence of the two provides a quick deep gravel run with sand rising up quickly towards the margins. Six to a dozen fish live in the hole gouged out by the current. They do move away sometimes, either forced out by a passing jack pike or by a clumsy angler; or at dusk to stray into the shallows above to do a little surface feeding. On the point of darkness, the fish often show briefly for insects about twenty yards from the hole and they might progress even further away in the hours of true darkness. These fish are not the largest in the stretch – probably the area is too small and fast to accommodate many large fish.

This small depression at the confluence quickly shallows out and for two hundred yards the river runs straight and featureless past a cottage garden and boat bay where a cat always sleeps to soak up the sun. Then comes the cattle drink, a big sand saucer cut into the banks which gives way to a shingle bottom and a decent drop off to four feet. There is always a reasonable steady flow over the swim which makes it attractive to those highly mobile shoals of dace that live in the shallows. It is not a place habitually lived in, but it is not unusual to see fish rise there at dusk or flash in the current during the day. A thorn tree marks the spot from a distance: a strange angular tree left with a yard of its roots exposed by previous floods, but still clinging into the sand and gravel soil.

The flood plain opens out wide from here, spreading away from the ridges, flat and green or deep ploughed brown into the misty distance, broken only by straggling dykes or wind blown hedges. Sometimes cattle graze, there might be a labourer somewhere to be seen, or an odd heron fishing a brook, but overall the place always looks bleak and empty. The only real life is given by the flocks of lapwings, always calling, or flying overhead with slow steady wing beats.

Their exotic white chest feathers gleam, even in February fogs and look too romantic for the drab English countryside.

Today, there are the skeletons of moles around in the wet grass: tiny bleached bones and scraps of dark skin with tight clenched paws and long shrew like noses. There was a flood last month and it would have chased them to the last, highest hillock and then still rising, would·have forced them to the highest molehill. And there they were drowned or eaten by the herons or the rooks and now they are picked clean.

Beneath the cattle drink, the river moves on a hundred yards to the first shallow bend. It is deepening and the current is slowing now all the while, dropping silt off over the gravel. Like the drink, it is a swim used often, but generally by smaller fish. Another eighty yards on though and the river turns into the Great Bend. Through the years this place has developed as a fish holding area as the Pool and the confluence have declined, until now there are always fish present and probably they are the biggest in the river.

The actual curve of the river takes about forty yards to complete: the flow declines noticeably with an uneven but

shelving bottom. The paths the currents take vary according to the rain fall and the winds, but a constant, deep slack exists on the outside of the bend and it is in this slack that the dace spend the bulk of their time. The bed here is surprisingly clean, generally sand and shingle, and the currents and back-currents continually drift food in from the main flow.

The dace here live very much like big roach, rarely coming far off the bottom, generally feeding deep, only sometimes at dusk and dawn rolling on the surface in splashy rises. Roach and chub do come into the bend with them for a while but whilst they move off the same dace shoal stays resident. There are about twenty fish – most big and some very big – spawned perhaps eight or nine years ago and having survived the menace of the odd travelling otter, herons, continually marauding jack pike, anglers, age and disease. This small dace shoal represents the peak of dace development for me and to tuck in behind the copse, settled behind the sedges waiting for dusk to come in and to see a big fish or two rise, is excitement indeed.

From the bend, the river runs away a hundred yards, shallowing all the time to the island. An old ox-bow has been created. On the one side a slow channel with varying depths; on the other the main river passes through in a faster, deeper run, until the two rejoin at the bottom end of the Island. Using all this water, lives a resident shoal of between twenty and thirty good fish.

In flood, they use the ox-bow, sheltering in the deeper pools along its course, but at other times they prefer the faster water either above or below the island. They make up one of the most visible shoals of fish, partly because they are relatively numerous, partly because they are large, but also because they move more on the surface than any other fish of the stretch. They are keen to come up to feed on floating bread or casters, whilst a west wind blowing a fly hatch off the marsh is never overlooked.

The island itself is a wild place, a confusion of willows and alders both growing and fallen in an uncared for jungle. The river is unbridged, years go by without a human setting foot on it and it has been claimed by the jays, owls and wood-peckers. On the western skyline is the church tower and the sun sets right behind it in the winter as the mists creep in and hide the Island and all but the tallest of the trees. It is a romantic place to be for a while.

Beneath the island, the river broadens sharply, the bends smooth away and there is less intimacy or character. For three hundred yards, the river is little populated other than by occasional passing roach shoals or nomadic chub, until on the right hand bank, we come to the delta. The entry of a side stream has over the years produced a large sweep of sand and shingle along the margins and three yards out until a sharp drop off falls to the true bottom. As the pool has declined as a fish holding piece of water and as the dace have begun to drop away from it downstream, they have tended to look for a new, more adjacent, less disturbed spawning ground and they have found it at the delta.

The dace gather there for a while in the spring, and though I have never seen them actually spawn there, their fry is quite visible over the sand by the late summer, harried by herons, frequent kingfishers and jack pike and occasional mature brown trout. These hang in the deep river, driving onto the delta at intervals, especially around dawn.

From what I see here on the Falls stretch, the dace is a struggling species. Abstraction, spawning sites under attack from canoes or dredgers or expanding communities, frequent pollution from expanding industry, the probability of harmful agricultural chemical inflows all make the future of the dace very uncertain. Certainly, very many of this country's south-eastern rivers hold nowhere near the number of sizeable dace that they did in the 1950s or 1960s.

Dace are attacked in so many low key ways. Hardly ever will their demise make a headline. For example, in the same river, below the Falls, some years ago a feeder stream was dredged. Work took place in May, at the most vital time for all the life that tiny water fostered. It happened to be an important, hereditary dace spawning site and the gravelly pool that the main river fish used was swept totally away with that year's eggs – and many of the adult fish. At the time, I grieved for the frogs, toads, newts, waterbirds as well as the dace and though the former have recovered, the dace in that beat of river never have.

Stillwater, freshwater species – carp, bream, tench, roach and rudd are comparatively secure in their future; brown trout, originally and in truth a river fish, are being helped by the growth of still water trout fishing; barbel and chub, real river fish again, are also under threat, but their size and glamour makes them more desirable than dace and more interest is taken in their re-stocking. It is the dace's problem that there are few men who love them and their loss is mourned only by the few. They are not large, they cannot, because of their size, put up dramatic fights, they do not taste good and so have no commercial value and because of all this, their habitats are pushed back further and further.

To me this is tragic for they deserve every bit as much of our attention as the whale, the otter, the panda or any other thing civilization looks in danger of destroying. I remember an especially harsh winter when lakes, rivers and every freshwater was suffering badly. I travelled across Norfolk to the little river, the Nar, and fished what had once been an important millpool.

The sunset was one of those dazzling affairs that only the cruellest of anti-cyclones can provide. It lasted for hours, changing from yellows to red, never throwing warmth, just stark light on a shivering land. The Nar's flood plain was frozen into icing as far as the eye could see and whilst the sun was still up, the frost coated hard on the rod and the line glued itself to the rings. The birds were already in the barebone wood – everything else had burrowed in for a dire night – when I caught a dace. At that moment, it was the most obliging, beautiful thing I could ever have hoped to see. It was as silver as the stars, it twinkled as bright as the frost, and then as I held it in my hand and the sun's last rays caught it, the scales turned to rose and flame. It was as beautiful and as worthy a fish as I have ever seen and one that would be impossible to re-create if ever lost.

6 · Eels

Like every other angler, I have watched eels in clear rivers; small fish swimming past, slipping their way upstream, always upstream, as they search for a place to live out the most of their lives. I made a huge catch of them, once, in my teens, on a lake whilst dusk fell and a thunderstorm began to develop. The more vividly the lightning flashed, the more the eels seemed to feed, and by midnight I had caught over twenty fish.

Since then I have read everything I could find on this strange species that is born somewhere in the Atlantic, rides in towards Europe on the currents and tides; that lives, feeds and matures in freshwater and then returns somewhere back into the ocean to breed.

A while back I met a commercial eel fisherman, a man who has caught eels for his livelihood. One night I helped him with his nets. I soon realized that I knew nothing.

We were on a wide reed fringed dyke that led eventually to a Broad lying away through the aldercarr. We met two hours before dusk and I watched as he prepared the nets he was to lay that night. They were the age old fyke nets that lead the investigating eels from chamber to chamber until they arrive pretty well trapped and entombed in the last compartment, the cod end. To find a way out of that prison is impossible and there they lie till the morning and the coming of their collector.

Whilst it was still light, he laid the nets in great heaps on the stern board of the rowing boat, told me to take the oars and lay me a course hard into the reed margins. I had to go quicker, an oars length from the fronds and he began to lay the nets overboard. Quicker still – the speed of the boat had to be great enough to pull the nets tight and I bent into it like a galley slave. I thrashed a hundred yards and then was directed to the other bank and in this way the nets zig-zagged down the creek. As the last fyke went over, he tied a marker to it to guide us back in the morning. But now it was almost dark and we made our way back to a marshman's hut on the waterfront, used only from time to time by these wanderers of the night.

Inside we settled on old sacks and the eeler pumped up a Tilly lamp for our light and warmth. I took out my payment for his knowledge: a full bottle of whisky mixed with ginger. The smell of it soon filled the hut.

'What can I tell you,' he asked.

'Everything. Everything you know. Just as it comes into your mind.'

He began to talk, just random ideas as they came into his head, and I copied them down fast as I could in the constantly flickering light from the lamp. This is an edited version of what he said:

He never lays his nets before April – even a warm March is not enough to heat the cold winter water up past the lowest eel movement point of 6°C. Once he tried netting in late March and caught nothing – though he could see their air holes in the mud where they lie the winter through in comparative warmth and safety. They are not completely secure because the cormorants and the grebes can pry them out of the silt and pike can dig them out if the winter gets cruel enough. Once April arrives with spells of warmer weather, and longer days, the water temperatures quickly rise and the eels become more active, but not until May do his quality bags come in.

May is a good month for another reason. On his waters the bream and roach spawn towards the end of the month. Indeed on one of the biggest lakes both species spawn on the 24 May every year. It does not matter how cold or warm the spring has been, on that day the cyprinoids begin to spawn. It has always been so. On another lake the fish are always six days later. He can set his plans rigidly to these dates and be on the water during the spawning time. This is vital. The spawning beds attract the eels from all over the broad – big

[66]

The Angler's Eel

and little eels alike worm their way to the mating grounds, and there they feast on the eggs. They eat them off the reed stalks, they ground themselves on the ronds after the washed up eggs, they eat them off the gravel and pick them up off the silt. They glide up to the convulsing fish themselves to eat the eggs as they shower from their very vents.

There, in amongst this chaos, the eeler puts down his nets. Sometimes the spawn gets into the fykes themselves and the eels will push themselves in to get at it there. Days after, long past the actual spawning time, the smell of the stuff on the nets still pulls the eels in. Yes, the May spawning days are the great haul times and on occasion the weight of the eels has threatened to sink his boat and stones of the fish have had to be shovelled back alive over the side.

Other than to get at the spawn, I could not understand why the eels should enter the nets at all. Some traps I could comprehend, like the dreaded, severed horse's head in Gunther Grass's *Tin Drum*, but what drives a fish to sacrifice itself to a barren net? Eels, the man said, like rubbing their bodies on a hard surface – that was why I had to row faster, to keep the nets tighter, so that the fish would follow the taut surface into the pokes right down to the cod end. That is why eels are attracted to the snagged areas of a water, where they can writhe against sunken trees, old machinery and sunken boats. A slack net will catch nothing.

Also, like duck decoys, eels attract other eels. If a few eels make their way into the pokes, then others are bound to follow. Indeed it pays to keep baskets of eels alive near the nets to call in free eels from around. Whether it is the smell, or the vibrations or whatever, I do not think anybody knows – but this is how it happens and how good catches of the fish are made.

Eels, the man said, do not move in the day, not decent eels of over 1lb anyway. A net left out from dawn to dusk will produce nothing. He knows, he had tried this and he is convinced the better eels lie quite dormant during the bright hours. Bream feed better at night but they do move in the daytime: not so eels. They are the bats of the fish world.

During June, July, August and September the eels move more freely and the higher the air and water temperatures rise the better they are caught. Despite my experience in thunder

[68]

those twenty years ago, the eeler has never noticed any real advantage in a storm, and puts it down to folklore and myth that the electricity excites the creatures. Cloudy, close nights are those that fill the nets and those with clear skies and big moons are invariably poor. Perhaps it is the cold that affects the water temperatures, but much more likely, it is the light that keeps the eels down.

Before their return to sea, before their mysterious migration back to the spawning grounds, strange things happen to the body of the eel. The fish begins to feed very hard, probably all through the high and late summer in order to put on weight and develop a thick coating of fat. Then in the months of September, October and November, the returning eels begin to run. For five nights in each month the run is at its height: for two nights before the last quarter of the moon, on that night itself and then for the two nights following it, the fish are on the move.

The fish are now silver in colour. They no longer feed. Their vents are sealed, in preparation, the eeler said, for becoming sexual organs when they reach the appointed place in the Atlantic. The silvers move in the first part of the night, before the small moon is up, when the light is at its lowest point. These fish on the run fear any light – a light on the bank, say a light in a Mill House, will turn them back to look for a different water course. The eeler told me of a dyke pump on one of his marshes that repeatedly jammed by silvers on the nights of the run, until the marshman put a lamp over the pump and kept it burning for all the five nights.

If the last quarter period coincides with wet weather, then the biggest nets are made. Endless deep depressions blown in from the Atlantic by stormy westerlies, in fact good stormy weather is what the eeler wants. Should the five nights be clear, frosty and still, the eels might not move but lie waiting in frustration. By November their urge to be gone could over-rule the state of the moon and if a spell of very wet weather and cloud covered nights sets in they will be driven to move on even the full phase.

Some nights, the eeler continued, he sets liggers, lines with floats and fifty or sixty baited hooks which the eels gorge. At

first he set the liggers so that the baits lay hard on the bottom and night after night he retrieved them fishless and unmarked whilst the old lads rowed past with full boats and laughed. He had to learn, had to, so he waited till past midnight and set off onto the broad to find the other mens' lines to discover their secret. It was nearing dawn before he ran upon Bertie's ligger and he held the lantern close to the water to study the rig carefully. The baits were all suspended just six inches from the surface and my eeler admits he laughed a good deal, for Bertie had obviously tangled up that night he thought. But, two hooks further along the line swam a hooked eel, and another, and more, and in fact, all but a ligger full of caught fish was awaiting Bertie in the sunrise. My eeler could not believe it. He thrust his oar down to the bottom and guessed it to be six feet down and yet these eels had come up to the surface layer to hunt and be caught. Some of the eels were big ones too, over 3lb, and not one of the baits had been left alone. He rowed, mystified, over the water towards his lines and pulled his fifty hooks off the bottom. Not a bait had been touched. He had learnt his lesson and the other boys never had a chance to laugh at him again on that score.

On the hooks he puts small dead fish, little perch are the winners, but never longer than 3in lest a jack come up to snaffle the bait and pull the ligger line off and away into the broad not to be seen again. Liggering works well all the summer, but not when the bream are spawning because the eels are on the bottom then gorging on the tiny eggs, not looking above their heads for larger foods. But anyway, it doesn't matter, because he doesn't ligger now – now liggering is breaking the law.

It was dawn by now and I think that we both felt bear headed through lack of sleep, the stuffiness of the shed and the amount of liquor, but the wind was still fresh and the clear stinging cold bit into our lungs, watered our eyes and swept a lot of the night away. There was something of a dew and we left dark tracks on the grass and it showered off the rushes onto our boots and overalls. He led me to the wall that separated the freshwater from the salting.

'I've never seen eels go overland,' he said, 'but one morning, very like this, that sluice gate down there got jammed

C TURNBULL 83.

Barbel

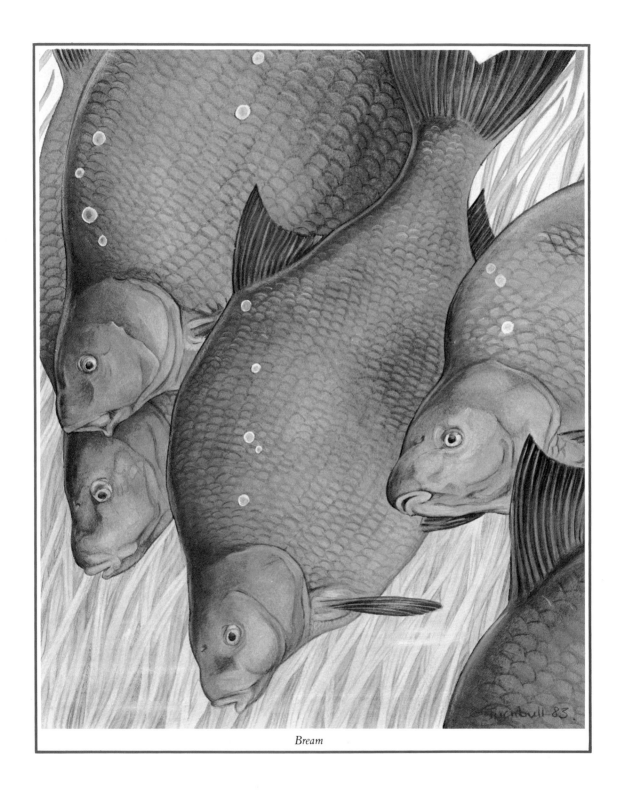

Bream

Carp

Crucian Carp

Chub

Dace

Eel

Perch

Pike

Roach

Rudd

Tench

up, all blocked by weed so that nothing could pass through. I came up here and saw their pathways through the dew. Doubtless they had been making for the sea and been forced up here to make a trek. I suppose they could not travel over dry ground, but the moisture made it possible for them. Mind – I've never seen the eel on the grass – just its tracks you know. I don't want to be written down for something I never said.'

We got to the boat and I rowed off to the marker where he threw out a hook – a crawler he called it – to hoist in the first net. I cannot deny that primitive instinct of excitement in me as I peered into the mist laid water, wondering what each net would hold, half tipping the craft over as I strained to see down into the depths. Some nets were quite empty and I cursed and swore whilst the eeler just hauled away. Others had a clutch of bootlaces in the pokes with a couple of decent fish in the cod ends, whilst some of the nets were just so full of eels it was a job to pull them over into the boat.

The man worked very hard and fast. As the nets were brought in, the cord tying the cod end was slipped and the catch fell through into a ten gallon pail. There was no water in the bucket. The fish writhed quite literally croaking in their own slime and gulping in the oxygen. In a cold misty atmosphere as hung around that morning the eels could live two hours at least without water – but if a covering of water got into the pail, then there would, he said, be deaths. As the eels thrashed and writhed they would lose their slime which mixed with the water combines into a mix of viscous suffocating fluid. Keep them dry he said.

All the while, the eels were throwing up the fish they had hunted that night before their imprisonment, and soon the water boards were a mortuary of little fish, mostly rudd and cocky ruffe, all 3 or 4in, quite fresh, unmarked but for a scuffing of the scales. Even a little eel managed to cough up a decent gudgeon. That eel went back. He was too small. Anything less than 6–8oz was returned. 'You've got to preserve the stocks. I'm rigid to that. We'd be fished out in a season if we took all and I aim to be here in this boat when we're both old, boy.'

I wonder now. Had I seen barbel, carp or bream dropped

[71]

into that pail then I would have cried out. Yet the eeler has been fishing years and his father a lifetime before that and the eels still come out as thick each spring as the last. He is part of that marsh world and deserves his life like every other predator in it, I suppose, and he certainly that night taught me about eels.

7 · Bayfield Perch

There is a lot in a name, especially a name that rings like Bayfield. An elegant hall stands there and a very beautiful valley lies beneath it through which runs the River Glaven, dammed to create a long, thin lake. At the bottom end there is a deep sluice where the water falls back into the old course and meanders away through the flint village of Glandford, under the Mill and along to Wiveton bridge and then to Cley and the sea. Around the sluices grows a good wood, mostly natural trees, but some planted ornamentals as though once the Lake were part of an impressively large garden. I cannot tell you how wonderful the whole place was in summertime when I used to fish there often: those warm evenings that gave into mild nights led tench to feed just as long as you wanted to stay there, and that would almost always be a long time.

But it was late one November that I made the discovery of perch at Bayfield. A village man and I were whiling away a few afternoon hours after roach when, at the same time, we both hooked big fish that we couldn't hold on light gear. Both fish got clean away but stayed quite long enough for me to realize neither roach nor tench were to blame and that perch were the only obvious culprits.

This was news and I set off to my fishing partner's cottage on the coast. Joe and I excitedly discussed plans, to set about catching these unexpected fish.

By Christmas time, we had had a lot of very big perch and loved Bayfield even more than we had done in the summer. The mild, misty autumn, the gentle early winter both gave the valley a softness, a mystery we both felt; we really believed that something exceptional could happen in that enchanted place. And, it very nearly did.

Christmas Eve, just past the shortest day, was hung with low clouds so that by early afternoon the light seemed all but gone. I was late arriving and Joe was already a black figure on the sluices with two fine perch in his net, so I settled beside him and cast two baits a rod length or so out under the draping trees. Down on the valley floor, in the wood there, the day was as good as dead, but mild with bats fussing in the gloom and the rooks drawing into the tallest trees.

We were talking, laughing, smoking a bit and I reeled in for another cast and found the fish already on and going like hell. Well, it went here and there and back again on a short line without me ever being able to do a thing to stop it. Joe lit a cigarette, smoked it and was into another before it began to surface. Of course, the light had gone, and dusk plays tricks – of course, after such a battle we both wanted to see something really big – but neither of us were expecting a perch quite as massive as that one rolling before the net. It came off. A swirl on the lead water where it had been and Joe smoked the cigarette out and I stood in silence. We took the tackle down and drove home.

I got into the study and took out a photograph of my grandfather taken back in Edwardian times, standing behind a table that groaned with pike (he took them to feed the Jews of Nottingham's poor quarters). But, as had been usual, those two months past, my gaze went straight to the perch that lay across full three of the pike, dorsal fin still defiant telling of the fighter in defeat or death, the mouth still gaping and the eye still wildly open. It had weighed over four pounds and did not go to the Jews but to the Taxidermist. My grandmother had given the case away in 1950, the year before I was born; but she could not have known that I would ever be a perch fisherman. My perch was not just as big as his but it was bigger. And just once, my voice back, I cursed very loud and still felt very little but despair. Yet deep down, a tremour of gratitude began to stir because it does not befall many men to have an excitement like that for ten minutes on a mystical Christmas night.

The loss of that big fish really drove me on: all the rest of that season I was like a wildman. I only dug early tides, and worked like a dervish so that I could be off the muds with a thousand worms and away perching for as much of the day as

The autumn perch lake

possible. Bayfield Lake, Worthing Pit, the Wensum, the Bure, Selbrigg Pond and many more – I fished them day, and day into night. I caught perch from them all, big perch, got my name in the papers for them, felt myself a celebrity for a while until I remembered that lost fish . . . and the satisfaction went.

Of course, I never landed a perch as big, or even ever saw one. Probably it grew in my mind as the obsession spread and got hold. Then, like all other perch fishermen everywhere, my hopes and plans were dashed and it seemed as if for ever.

THE DISEASE

In July I visited Worthing Pit after a night of heavy rain and winds. During March before, I had three big perch and now I had a bucket of small livebaits with me hoping for a summer fish. The wind had blown directly the length of the pit, heaping all before it into the bay at the southern end, and that is where I made for.

Broken reeds, washed up weed, a couple of bottles and other litter rocked in the dying waves, and there also in the surf lay two big perch. Dead. Ulcerated. Stirred up by the storm and left there on the shallows as a stark message of what had befallen the pit. The perch disease had hit. I did not have the stomach to fish that day but walked around and around the perimeter of the water and found other smaller fish, in the rushes, stranded on the gravel, all but one dead, and that one died literally as I watched.

Since, I have read reports of the perch disease and have seen photographs, but to see the fish you have so cared for actually struck down is a far more powerful memory. The lesions cut through the flesh to the very bone: the buccaneer stripes of that most handsome fish are lost in bloodied, scattered scales. The posterior flanks of the perch were all but rotted and in some fish the fins themselves were bleeding with open sores.

By the end of that summer, I felt sadly sure that all my previous winter's perch waters had suffered similarly and though I fished determinedly until the following Christmas, I didn't see one big fish, or come to that, any perch at all.

A swim on the River Wensum especially indicated the fate that had befallen, seemingly overnight. Not on one session before had I failed to catch decent perch, but now the area was devoid of them – apart from one carcass I saw 4ft down on a sand bar. It had wedged across some weed where a shoal of sticklebacks was pulling at a flap of skin, dislodging flesh from time to time, each bit being chewed and tugged in midwater.

Bayfield has never fished for perch again as far as I know, and though it has been made a good tench water once more, I do not suppose Joe and I will ever sit by the sluice come winter. The Bure perch simply vanished without any trace. One or two dead perch were found at Selbrigg Pond, simply representatives, I am sure, of the rest that lay dead beneath the weed. But, of course, perch wipe-outs of these proportions were in no way unusual and in retrospect I was very fortunate to get that last winter in. My Bayfield perch days were on borrowed time and East Anglia had in fact been one of the last regions to contract the Perch disease that devastated most of England at least two years earlier.

The first recorded epidemic hit Windemere in 1964, returning in 1965. In 1967 severe fatalities took place in the Metropolitan reservoirs and Abberton, and a year later Pitsford, Ravensthorpe, Hollowell, Grafham, Manningfield and Windermere again all lost a lot of fish. Indeed in Windermere, an estimated 98 per cent of perch stocks were lost and it seemed that no sexually mature fish at all had survived.

Even now, the cause of the Perch Disease has yet to be satisfactorily established. Research shows that a virus is unlikely to be the cause and more probably one of the *aeromomas* bacteria is involved in some way. These bacteria are, however, endemic in our waters, so the disease is unlikely to be transmitted by angler's tackle or waterfowl; more probably a combination of factors occurs to act as a catalyst on a normally inactive causative agent. If this is not the case, then conditions stress the perch and render them vulnerable to infection. Weather conditions, pollutants, the increased entrophication of lowland waters, or any other factors could combine to affect the perch and promote the possibility of disease.

But nature recovers. It is resilient. Some perch always managed to survive the Disease and re-occurring incidences do seem to be more sporadic without bringing about the massive fish kills of the 60s and 70s. Possibly, perch will react to ravaging disease like rabbits have adapted to myxomatosis. Though no fully resistant strain of rabbits has emerged yet, there is evidence that they are building up immunity and we can hope the same evolutionary process will take place with perch.

THE 1980s: THE PHOENIX PERCH

Big perch then, faded into the memory like a place once visited but never forgotten and other species filled the time. Perch articles came and went in the angling press, generally with old photographs, written by over optimistic men out to make a buck or a name by preaching that tired 'perch revival' message.

And then, nearly ten years on, there came true whispers on the wind, and then, one February, rumours so strong that they had to be checked out. After noon on a clear, cyclonic day with an unclouded sun and a little breeze from the North, a gudgeon livebait was working alongside a reed bed, quite on fire in the bright light. Pessimism had crept in, for surely it was too late in the day for perch action, and the rumour had turned out to be nothing but that. The children were playing in the farm yard, had ignored the third call to lunch; farm workers' cars were leaving the pub on the other side of the lake and a short lazy afternoon seemed to be started when the float went and the line gushed down the rod rings.

Five minutes later, there was much rejoicing on the bank and you felt like pinching yourself out of the dream that produced a perch like this one, so perfect in fin and scale with no scars or ulcers on its fifteen inch flanks. From that day, other perch waters came back into being and the things that I had known about the species were valid once more.

Not every water can produce big perch, and though nearly all English freshwaters will produce small ones, particular circumstances are needed for them to grow. First, the water must have enough small fish for the 5–6in perch to be able to supplement his insect diet with fish and grow into that next dimension, the predatorial perch. If just a few perch can get to 12oz in weight, then they are able to turn onto their small brethren, become cannibal and then their emergence into 2lb plus fish is virtually assured. Minnows, sticklebacks, gudgeon, loach or fingerlings of any species act as the first fish diet that a few of any perch year class will profit from. Not every perch in a group will turn predator and those that remain on a small food diet will never grow above a few ounces, and may be eaten.

Sometimes a natural fluke will help a group of perch burst through into the predatorial bracket. For example, a particular lake held only large, seemingly sterile carp and small perch. There were no other small fish of any type at all and for years the perch averaged only three or four ounces. One July, however, quite unexpectedly, the carp spawned freely, producing many thousands of fingerlings which were eaten by a small percentage of the perch. Within a few months these carp eating perch had grown enough to tackle the 2oz fish of their own species and comparatively shortly, the pool held a moderate stock of big perch.

Every water where perch have been successful has to my certain knowledge had a good head of small fish. I can see no

way round this. It must be so. Let me tell you the story of J.D.'s ornamental fishpond. This, on the veranda of his house, was greatly overstocked with tiny roach of only three or four inches, and so when another pool on his estate was being netted, he transferred four of the 1lb perch that were caught into this fishpond. All was quiet in the fishpond over the next two years; he then noticed that the number of roach had decreased dramatically and so, one night, he decided to put a spinner down the 4yd water. The first troll produced a take and a perch of 4lb 2oz.

Secondly a good perch water must be a clear water. It should be clear in the summer and for as much of the winter as possible, and the reason is simple. Perch hunt fish predominantly by sight and though they might pick up the proximity of a fodder shoal through the senses, the actual kill is by chase and capture. A water that clouds up for much of the year simply cuts down on the length of time that a perch is feeding and growing. There are exceptions to this rule – I know of one big perch water where visibility is rarely more than 9in, and there must be a few others, but certainly in my experience clear waters are in by far the majority.

Thirdly, perch do flourish in water that is to an extent saline. One of my finest perch waters was the River Glaven, and the best swim was actually at the sluice gates where the river met its estuary. It is possibly the effect of the salt that promotes growth, or perhaps the very rich feeding on prawns, elver runs and the like, but the slightly saline waters of all Europe do produce some of the best perch.

In summer, perch seem to feed best at dawn, sometimes at dusk, and occasionally on a dull day or in the shade of trees or thick weed. By the autumn, on most waters, the perch will feed well in the daytime on the fry of that summer. Fry driving periods last for up to half an hour and then there will be a quiet of an hour or so for digestion before the cycle is repeated three or four times in the day.

By winter, the perch are becoming less active and their feeding spells grow shorter and less frequent. Each water develops its own pattern, but dawn after the first hard frosts is nowhere near as favoured as before, and, countrywide, a feeding period becomes increasingly likely any time between

10am and 2pm. Last light in winter takes over from dawn as the prime feeding time and the perch will carry on feeding into darkness. That perch feed by the light of the moon in all seasons is now well known: a big moon is thought best, shedding the light that a sight hunting fish will obviously need.

A hunting perch hangs below its prey and then attacks upwards at an angle towards the posterior of the fish. It will chase its victim for yards, locked onto that particular fish, not veering off after others on its course. It will snatch and tug at the caudal fin of the fleeing victim, bit by bit cutting down its swimming capacity and ability to escape. When the prey has slowed sufficiently, then it will be taken tail first. At this point, the perch generally turns it and swallows it head first, though this is not always the case. Perch do not take their prey crossways, like pike.

The hunt is most spectacular when the perch is fry driving – the bow-wave and aggressively erect dorsal fin cutting the surface of the water whilst a fingerling skips ahead – which has become one of the most cherished sights in angling. So savage is the chase that the small fish will flee into shallows only inches deep and even beach themselves in an effort to escape.

Perch do not always hunt fry: they will lie up to ambush bigger fish that pass through gaps in the weeds, or follow trails through sunken tree roots. For its size, a perch has a cavernous mouth, and is quite capable of eating another fish a third of its own weight. This means that a big perch is quite capable of dealing with good roach or rudd, or in a river, decent dace, or even small chub.

The eating capacity of perch I find quite staggering. For a while I kept two small perch in an aquarium, fish that were quite content to eat maggots, worms, beetles, and other standard foods. Then, on the river, I netted out a shoal of small minnows, sixty or seventy in all, 2in fish, which I transferred to the tank. Immediately, the two partners took up hunting positions and harried those minnows up and down until, within forty eight hours, a mere half a dozen remained. These became increasingly difficult to catch, hiding for long periods, and lasted the best part of a month, falling one by one. Those minnows brought out the real buccaneer in the perch, showed

them to be real hunting fellows, with their fins up and quivering. The whole pulse rate of the tank rose: the dace and roach became more agitated, and frustrated by an escaping minnow, a perch would often have a go at a gudgeon in reality far too big for it.

Up to very large sizes, perch are a true shoaling fish. The largest fish become increasingly isolated as the fellows of their year class die away, and when left alone, the survivor does not always join in with a shoal of smaller perch. A perch shoal is a very close knit group: it hunts with an element of co-ordination between the different fish that make it up. It develops a long standing holding area where all the perch spend non hunting time. In lakes and pits, those deeper bays, surrounded by overhanging trees and bushes, thick on the bottom with silt and rotting branches, are the likely haunts of a perch shoal. They are the very last places that bream or roach or rudd would choose, but the perch love the shade and the camouflage.

In winter, the perch shoal will begin to look for the deepest holes in the lake, and will often go down to 40ft or more and hide down there all the cold weather through. From all these lairs, the perch shoal will make forays along certain patrol routes. The paths of the hunting shoal is not always the same one and varies as the seasons change. The perch simply know where to expect food fish at certain times of the year and make for these general areas by the shortest possible way. Once in the area, the shoal will home in on its prey partly by sight and partly by sensing the movement of the fry shoal it seeks.

River perch behave in very similar ways. They too like their hole up spots to be undisturbed and avoid the fast streamy water in favour of deeper, clearer water. Every river has its legendary perch hole and my best one ever was a deep calm eddy that had thick, ivy strewn bushes growing over it. The combination of slow water and cover proved irresistible and shoal after shoal would take up residence until anglers scared them on. Close by, the deeper water gave way onto gravel shallows, paved with minnows, loach and gudgeon, and here the shoals fed.

8 · *Pike*

A BROADLAND MORNING

There is a knot of cottages I have been to, some thatched, a little flint walling but mostly old red brick. They stand around a green and lie a couple of miles down a single track road. Boats stand in the gardens in winter and in their sheds lie scythes, fish nets, duck decoys, skates and rods. The guns, the cartridges, the precious things of Broadland stay indoors. Nothing much has changed in a century or so, I suppose, and the only engine you are likely to hear on a Sunday is a chainsaw. I mention all this simply to show parts of the wilderness as it was, do still exist.

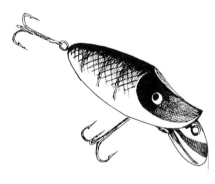

If you go over the stile and through the wood, a shooter's wood thick in ash and alder, oak on the drier soil and a ground cover of buckthorn and guelder rose, you will come to the Broad. A wild fowler's Broad where once a gun punt was used and the carcass of it still remains, sunk to the gunnels in the boatshed with the swivel that once took the weapon just above the waterline now.

We take a punt that is not a lot better and needs a lot of bailing, but get out on to open water as it is coming light. There is a high wind over the county, but the forest keeps if off us here and the rowing is not too difficult, even though the clouds really scud past in the blue sky. We move here and there, fishing all the while, trying most things a pike fisherman knows: a couple of livebaits search along the reeds, deadbaits lie on the bottom, and two plugs dither and dive along radiating lines back to the boat. A pike strike is what we need to see and home onto, for in pike fishing location is everything, absolutely everything.

Chris Turnbull 85.

It seems colder with the sun on the tree line than it was before and the wind does feel keen. We stand up in the boat and beat our arms to keep warm and then bail out more of the skim-iced water. It is Broadland and so there are birds everywhere, coots, as usual, fighting and the water hens looking on through the reeds. Wherever we move a new drape of ducks lifts off the water as we approach: a woodpecker sounds above the wind, the jays catch the sunlight and the tits and finches are busy in the reeds.

It must have been nine before we saw sign of pike, and then they were fry feeding. A volley of strikes hit the fingerlings that had been herded into a cove, so we heaved in the mud-weight and got up there amongst them all, because, after all, location is everything.

The water is shallow and clear and as we watch we see pike coming into the food, lifting the fry up to the surface, taking those that they can and getting back to the mouth of the bay both to chew and digest and also to keep the shoal tethered whilst other pike take their feeding turn. We put what baits we

have out over the area, but do not get a single take because after all, fry feeding pike become as preoccupied as barbel over hemp and our herrings must look quite ludicrously large to them in such a mood. Still, it is good to be above fish, some of them nice ones and all the while it is developing into one of those miracle days that February can sometimes conjure up. As the wind drops and the sun gets up, the temperatures rise enough to bring flies out over the reeds where the small birds begin to swarm.

But we keep moving, half an hour here and a few casts there and by lunchtime we find some fish. The red float tips up and the line draws tight over the water and I strike down into a dour fight that begins to get really lively near to the boat, when the pike can see the net looming close.

HICKLING BROAD

In December 1982, I spent all the month on the ocean of water created by Hickling, Heigham Sound, Horsey Mere and the River Thurne, an area of hundreds of acres of water and reed swamp, with no human habitation and roads no more than tracks, where oars are more use than wheels and wings are faster than either. It was a cold month and on only one day that I fished, did temperatures get above 7°C. Strong or gale force winds were normal and once even overland the gusts were into storm. Despite these winds, there were frequent frosts and because of them, the tidal push up the River Thurne was often very heavy, flooding out over the towpath and into the marsh. I was generally alone and I really loved the place, so flat with a vastness of skyline and the sugar mountain clouds piled up over the sea to the north and east. Most evenings became clear with a darkening sky and a setting sun that cast a brilliant light on to the swamps of marsh and reed. All day long, straggling cormorants would have battled overhead, but come dusk there was a constant passage of ducks and geese and any lull in the wind let in the cries of the herons in the Hickling roost. Over the Sounds, from there patrolled the pair of marsh harriers, quartering the dykes around Stubbs Mill and off into Horsey. Fabulous birds that hung on the wind like paper kites.

When you take a boat from Martham Ferry, head west and

then turn north up Candle Dyke, you begin to sense another world, and when you pass the old eel set and the hunting lodge on the corner and get into the southern fringes of the Sound, you know you are really there.

A clear calm afternoon in winter is the time to be best aware of the vastness up there, of those great sheets of water and the reed swamp pitted with bays and pools and channels where a man could quite get lost if a mist came down. This Hickling Ocean, taking in the Sound and the Mere, has produced more big Pike than any other single water in England, and fleets of famous men have rowed and fished here: Peter Hancock who caught the English record; Denis Pye, the best known pike

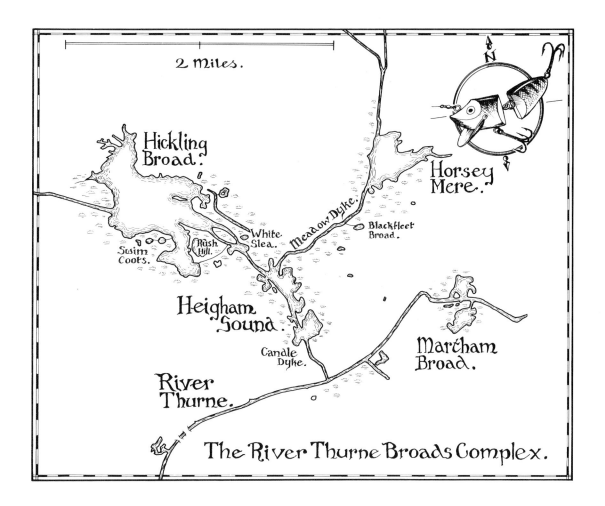

angler of the 1960s; the brilliant boat fishing duo of Bill Giles and Reg Sandys; Frank Wright; and many more who have come and been successful.

MASTER OF THE HICKLING OCEAN

There is a man who knows the Ocean as well as anybody else and probably loves it more; he sees himself as an heir to a lot of knowledge of the waters there and to hear him talk about it with such enthusiasm and feeling, is a pleasure. This knowledge he possesses has been amassed over three generations that he knows about, and probably started even further back.

Jim Vincent, a Hickling man, born in 1884, was a professional wildfowler and eel catcher, and by 1909 the gamekeeper of the White Slea Lodge Estate that covered the Ocean. He was brought up in a hard world where, as his son Edwin wrote 'the spoils go to the experts', and Jim could not afford not to know all about the fish and birds of his marsh world. Certainly, long before his death in 1944 he knew the traditional haunts of the big pike.

This knowledge was passed on to Edwin and to his friend Denis Pye and their catches filled the headlines of the 1950s and 1960s. Although some doubt has been cast on some of Denis' records, that he caught a huge total of big fish, and that he knew the location of the pike intimately, cannot be denied. He could also be generous and he frequently took a young man with him in those great days, Derrick Amies, to whom he passed on piece by piece the knowledge.

In the late 1960s, *prymnesium* struck all the Hickling area. *Prymnesium* is not a disease, but a poisoning of the fish caused by a microscopic plant or alga which lives in salt or brackish water and which under favourable conditions multiplies rapidly to produce a dense algal bloom. Chemicals released by the bloom contaminate the water and poison all the fish in the area by rendering the gills permeable to a wide range of toxic substances such as copper, which cannot normally enter into the system of the fish. It also kills by causing the cells of fish, especially the red blood cells, to disintegrate.

Fish can at times sense the poison and evacuate the area for fresh water in time to save themselves. Bream and roach shoals are adept at this moving away as members begin to die, but the pike being a more solitary fish, does not have the same warning and suffers more. Certainly, by winter 1969, the vast majority of pike in Hickling, Heigham and Horsey were dead and that second generation of pike anglers stopped fishing there.

In the 1980s, Derrick again rose to fame with fabulous catches from these waters once more. The pike had recovered, and though they were still very far from being plentiful, they had remained massive fish, far beyond the experience of normal pike anglers. And Derrick knew where in these hundreds of acres of water to find them. Denis had taught him what winds to look for, how to spot a far off bream shoal and all the things that a Master of the Ocean would need to know. The new Master because Denis was by now dead.

The Hickling complex is a pike water on the grand scale, and it ranks with the Scottish Lochs or the Shannon System as an entire environment where the fish are blessed with a mass of alternatives for their lives. There, a pike can find any depth it wants, great or shallow, and the food supplies and the flow it

desires – from still to swift – and the type of shelter it seeks in countless bays and reed margins. There is really an underwater universe for the pike to use exactly as they need it. By comparison, the pike of a pond or a small pit are more like goldfish, without any real choices to make or chance to develop. As Derrick says, to know pike on a water like Hickling is to know pike as they want to be.

The Hickling pike date back to the thirteenth century when the medieval peat diggings were flooded by a series of severe storms, and over the centuries they have adapted totally to this environment and are very efficient users of it. Nature has fashioned them into a rhythm and a pattern of life that is very much their own.

Autumn is the crucial period for the pike, as the boat traffic peters away quickly through September and as October falls over the Flats, the open expanses of water making up Hickling, Horsey and the Sounds. These vast sheets of shallows lie open to the Northerly and Easterly winds, exposed to the first frosts and sleet rains. Temperatures fall quickly and by November the roach and bream are moving in their thousands off the flats into the River Thurne, heading for deeper water and into the boat basins. For them the two or three foot flats are no place to be when the winter sets in.

Certainly by December, there is probably not a roach on Hickling: now the matches are won from Candle Dyke Corner and down into Potter Heigham. On 20 December 1982, I watched a cormorant hunting on the corner and it took a bream of a pound and left satisfied. Thereafter, on the calm days, at dusk, bream always topped there well into the New Year happily in the 6ft swim in a decent push of water.

Above all, these pike do not act haphazardly, they are deliberate in their movements and all their actions have a deep-rooted purpose which is why so many anglers fail to catch them. They believe their approach is penetrating and thoughtful where in fact it is only scraping at the surface of their behaviour and the pike and their pursuers never really interlock. The knowledge that Derrick Amies possesses looks into what the pike do. They are not intelligent or clever fish but simply act out the roles set for them over the centuries. From time to time anglers do stumble on to a part of the secret and then these big fish are caught, and very often suffer for they are very much more vulnerable than the majority of men think. The only enemy pike have is the pike angler and it is good that more and more careful pike handlers are spreading their message and techniques wherever they go.

But, and here is the crux of Derrick's knowledge, the pike do not follow the food fish. Of course some might, probably the smaller fish, but the majority of the biggest pike stay where they are and do not follow the roach and bream. More than that, it is precisely because the food shoals go that the pike remain. Early in the winter, they make for their spawning grounds on the Flats where their eggs will be produced safe in the absence of the roach and bream that would otherwise use them as a valuable food supply through the winter.

The Hickling pike have fed well in the summer and early autumn and have built up large enough reserves of body weight to keep them through a winter of limited feeding. Some are massive fish and do not need regular food – as the temperatures drop they begin to lie more torpid sometimes under ice on a simple tick over rhythm. As a mild spell develops, especially with rain and strong westerlies, then the pike do begin to stir and move – they will be gathered together in small bays, lined up like soldiers and agitation in the area will rise as they flicker more and more into alertness.

Derrick has watched this awakening of the giants, as their fins begin to quiver and their bodies ripple. Can't you imagine their eyes rolling and the adrenalin beginning to work through them? Accompanying jacks of up to six or seven pounds will be snapped at, seized across the flanks and they will struggle violently perhaps to tear themselves free and move off bleeding. Others will be eaten. A fish, probably a male which will be smaller, will be slashed at by a bigger female, perhaps three or more times his size and it might lose chunks from its back and have its stomach wall ripped. Two of the monsters might tackle each other, like dinosaurs of old, ripping wildly until they disengage and slide off into the silt cloud. In the skirmish, an eel might have been disturbed from the mud and out of nowhere a pike will be up to it and it will disappear into nowhere. Any coot or dabchick overhead at these wakenings might go down into a black hole that opens beneath them,

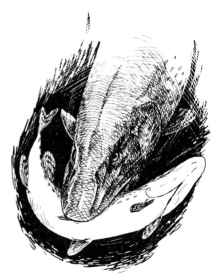

leaving only a few feathers spinning on a vortex of steadying water. Imagine being an angler present at these times, as Derrick often has been himself.

Could you keep calm? Could you steady your fingers as you hook on a smelt or a half herring to lower into the bay? Would you remember to check your knots and trace wire and make sure the net was spread ready? What would you think if you glimpsed something of a shadow, the size of a crocodile coming at the bait and then saw the float tip, and begin to move off under? I wonder if you could stop such a fish from the reeds for so enraged in such shallow water they go as if you had a tiger by the tail, and how would you feel if the pike got there and like a crashing fury broke you? But above all, what would you do if you got such a monster into the boat, when it dawned on you that here was a fish bigger than most men ever dream of, and it is going dark, miles from witnesses? Would you have the bigness of character to weigh it and release it unharmed, forsaking public acclaim but happy in the knowledge that such a great fish lived on? Derrick did just this very thing. He put back a pike of over 41lb.

LOCATION

I have said before that location in pike fishing is everything and the question rises as to why so few coves are haunted by the pike. Why on these huge sheets of water, with a thousand seemingly identical bays, do pike choose just a handful of them and largely neglect the rest? There is no doubt that the knowledge Derrick holds has these places marked down: he knows where the traditional spawning grounds are, those that the pike have used for generations. The bays are possibly rotated year to year, but the same few are chosen from and used frequently, but what marks them out, we can only guess at.

John Nunn lives right on an arm of Ormesby Broad and has over the years studied the nature of the banks there. On the softer banks where the water gradually shallows great reed encroachment takes place, ever accelerating as the dying vegetation add to the silt and peat, reducing even more the amount of water and providing still better growing

Pike on!

conditions. Pike undoubtedly like to lie in these reed jungles and get a long way into them off the main body of water. Such areas are promising.

On other lengths of bank, certainly on the Ormesby group of Broads, the peat was cut from out of a harder bank which has kept better its original contours. The sheer drop off here has meant that the reeds have not ever been able to get a hold and they look more barren and less interesting. However, over the years, undercuts have been worn into them, often stretching several yards under the reed fronds behind. How these undercuts have been created is in itself a puzzle. Perhaps at periods the water level has been lower and the wave action has eroded the now submerged waterline. More probably, on such large expanses of water, undertows of great strength build up and these pulls of current could eat at the less secure footings of the bank to produce these horizontal mine shafts.

What is sure is that pike use these undercuts widely as shelter and possibly as ambush areas if food fish should come past. In them the water will be darker and less disturbed and will never freeze, a fact important on the Flats, and yet the undertow will still maintain a circulation of oxygen and water. This push of water seems favoured by Broads fish and if the undercut is beneath a promontory where the sweep of bank accentuates the movement, so much the better. Similarly, John has found that pike will tend towards the mouths of feeder streams and where dykes empty in to the Broad.

Not all pike will be in the reed margins or in undercuts and the skirts of overhanging trees and bushes are important areas, particularly where the tangle of branches reaches deep into the water itself. During October and November the pike are probably here for the summer's fry shoals (that seek shelter in such places) and by January and February the attraction of the branches is as a spawning bed.

Away from the bankside, depth changes and ledges must play some part in pike location; so too do dormant weed beds and though they are submerged in winter and decaying, they will provide those threefold virtues – ambush and spawning site potential together with shelter.

A wood, Derrick Amies once told me, only holds so many owls. The rest either want, or are forced to leave, and so it is with pike. Many live the year out on the flats, but others, whilst perhaps using them in the summer, migrate in the winter on to the River Thurne. During my period fishing the area, four pike that I knew of over 25lb were taken there, and several others not much smaller. My feeling was that these fish, unlike those of the flats, were more nomadic and followed the fodder fish, frequently raiding the bream and roach holding areas. Certainly a length of river would produce fish for a while and then would die totally as a pike pack drifted away.

9 · *Wensum Roach*

On 24 October I went back to the site with Chris and Sharon. We bundled into the van and made the twenty mile journey on a near perfect autumn afternoon to this, most deserted of river stretches. Chris came because he wanted the inspiration for his drawings, the precision of details, the sense of the mood and feel of the place. Sharon came with me because we both love the memory and the look of a river that gave me a very definite place in angling history. Rarely, if ever before, had so many big roach come from one place in such numbers – and there were only two anglers on the water, me and J.J. – so the whole episode was unique and special.

Though it is six, or even seven years, since I have fished the swims with the dedication I showed then, the river has not changed, or at least not visibly. We sat on the hill that looks down the valley and the river was meandering away into a vivid sunset. I felt puzzled, wondering how to write this episode that meant so much and which is, I believe, very important and how not to distort those remarkable periods. I realized that I must use diaries, refer to my old notes to try to tell it as it was and not how my imagination or memory might have reshaped it since.

Chris walked up and down, round and round, planning pictures and I could tell the place had got to him. I pointed to the reeds where I stumbled upon an otter's tracks around a 3lb roach. The fish was freshly dead, but with its stomach shredded and, after making sure it was dead, I had walked away upstream hoping that the beast would return and would spare others.

I showed him J.J.'s swim, one of the strangest on the entire river. I remembered how I had found it, one cold February before either J.J. or I was married and when we both lived in a cottage by the river. It had been a bad time, as things were when we could not fish. The east wind blew through the windows and blew down the chimneys and piled the sky up with snow filled clouds. Yet, just as the afternoon light was teetering, I felt I had to fish, so I took down a pike rod and stumped off towards the river.

I started at the bridge, moving steadily upstream as the gloom settled and bedded in for the night. I had worked a mile: a storm was obviously near, the sky was that menacing colour of cygnet's down, when I got into the lee of a small island. The river looped behind it, where I could not reach, but the main push came down on my bank and I cast again. It was seconds before the tumbling copper spoon found bottom. Twelve feet deep I calculated. So strange when all the grey water upstream and down was only three or at the most four feet. There was no bend, no weir, no sign of the dredger, nothing to explain this great crater in the river bed.

[97]

I was thinking as the vast snow cloud broke and the flakes fell like melting moths into the water. I thought as I sheltered in the creaking, wind blown chicken shed. And then, as the light yellowed from white to gleaming ivory and darkened into a pale night, I realized that at least, I had found a potentially great swim.

J.J. fished the hole for five weeks and caught a massive bream there, and later in the spring, I discovered the reason for the whole thing. The site was an ancient watermill. It dated from as early as the tenth century perhaps, but was burnt down sometime in the fourteenth. Yet, six centuries had not served to destroy or silt the medieval mill pool. That isolated swim was a thousand years old.

Back in the present, the three of us walked the hundred yards or so upstream to the swim I had fished in that period. Once more the look had hardly changed. The sedges were browning, the bridge across the dyke had never been repaired and the river itself just wound past as slowly and placidly as it had always done along these reaches. There was no sign of anybody having fished it or even been there at all. It was as deserted and as neglected as when J.J. and I were on it.

We waited till the sun had sunk right down, watching the afterglow merge into the blue night sky, and the fire in the west, gradually give way to the starlight.

'Do you think there are still fish here,' Chris said simply. It was dark and time to go.

'I really don't know,' I replied.

This river, the Wensum, found me, of course. I did not find it. I was in no way at the forefront of opening the place up or finding its incredible fish stocks. In the 50s and 60s it had been well known and well fished and by the 1970s when I first really got close to it, it was already on its way to becoming a legend. But, in most places, the fishing was always hard and the upper river was never heavily fished. Certain stretches were renowned for their difficulty, with few or wary fish in them, and as a result were next to never tried. Indeed, on the island beat that I have mentioned, I never saw another angler – or even another human being – other than J.J. and very occasionally some angler invited along by us.

This is what makes my stay on the river here so important. I

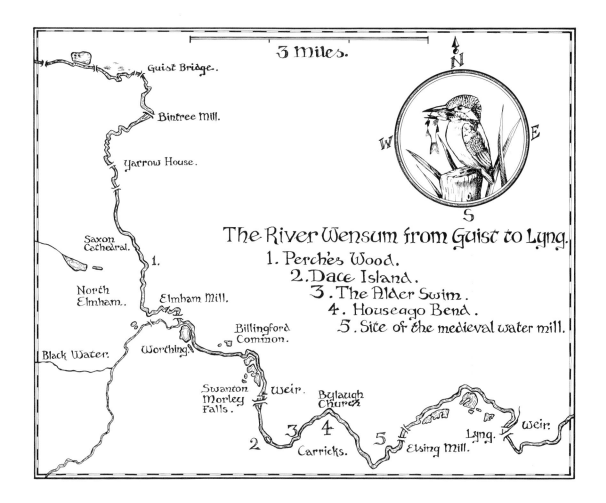

The River Wensum from Guist to Lyng.

1. Perch's Wood.
2. Dace Island.
3. The Alder Swim.
4. Houseago Bend.
5. Site of the medieval water mill.

believe it is the only time in angling history – or one of the very few times – that very, very big roach have been studied in an almost totally unharrassed, unspoilt, natural environment. Because there was so little human pressure, there was little likelihood that the fish were being disturbed, or were acting in any way differently to their normal behaviour. Whenever I saw fish, they were unhurried and deliberate; not the neurotic, scary fish of a heavily pressured environment. A fear of man did not really exist, or at least there was next to no recognition of man. Those fish had no knowledge of man – though of course they were still very shy of footfalls, shadows or any sudden movements.

[99]

Equally, the fish were naive towards baits. Their reaction to new, angler introduced food was very mixed. Used only to natural foods they took a long time to accept bread which was the staple bait we used at that time.

And what fish those roach were. I do not know exactly why I felt that this stretch of the river should produce better fish than others, but in part, it was a hunch. So deserted, so beautiful in a melancholy way, spiritually it felt right. More realistically, it had once held very large fish stocks but then, in 1967–68, the disease *columnaris* had attacked it, killing off the vast majority of the roach population. Had any fish survived, I felt that with the much reduced pressure on food supplies, they could become very big roach. Added to this, there were hints and rumours of roach still present and the river was immensely rich in shrimps, beetles, snails and bloodworms to sustain them. And then, finally, I had seen that otter eaten fish.

What fish those apparent survivors were. Scale readings in 1974 and 1975 put them at between 9 and 11 years but I am convinced they were older fish and the scales simply reflected their growth period, not their actual age. They were certainly fish that had lived through the disease: the first very large roach I caught just before Christmas 1974, I described then as 'like other survivors of the disease I had seen, its scales were terribly mutilated. Those it had left were jumbled and jagged, bits of fins had vanished. A deep old scar ran across its skull and along its shoulders where either a heron, a cormorant or an otter had once attacked it. It was an exciting fish to look at, thinking about its desperate, dangerous past and the massive size it had endured to.' Other fish were hideously malformed with open bleeding sores that had never healed and were still eating the fish away. A handful of fish had had their whole skeletons twisted until they revolved rather more than swam in the water and looked more like a boomerang or even a banana.

From what I saw over a three year period, these large, older fish never went up to the top shallow areas of the stretch to spawn in the springtime. The gravel beds and faster water they might have looked for were two miles distant but from what I witnessed they never left the sluggish, deep, silt covered areas nearest to the bottom mill. When roach were spawning in the tails of mill pools elsewhere, these big fish remained aloof and inactive. Perhaps the disease affected their fertility or perhaps their advanced age had had the same effect.

The roach moved in very small shoals. It has long been suggested that a year group of shoaling fish – roach and bream say – swim together as an entity and as the years and different dangers cut them down, the shoal simply gets smaller until it finally disappears altogether. This theory has never been better illustrated to me than when I was fishing for shoals of four, three, two or even one fish, the remnants of four figure strong groups probably, in the early sixties. I still find it rather sad that in the very early days of this period, I as yet did not realize quite the roach I was dealing with. I confess that I did sometimes keep a fish in a net over night for a dawn photograph and I am sure with hindsight such treatment did such a roach harm. But fish handling like this was quite common then and I am pleased that I quickly realized how irreplaceable and vulnerable they were and soon began to return the roach relatively untouched and unharmed to the river.

The big roach rolled at dawn and dusk and they made a very exciting sight. Trying to describe the action in words is quite impossible, trying even to visualize it and remember it in detail is well nigh impossible also, and makes me realize how hard a job Chris Turnbull has in trying to draw these things. They are movements of a milli-second: you can believe that they happened in a twinkling of an eye or that you even imagined it. I well remember the first big roach I saw roll at the island swim, but still all that I can do is describe the picture in general rather than in minute detail.

The late part of the night had been cold and there was a fair frost when I walked the river about 6 am. The banks were a silvered white with the browns of the sedges pushing through – the river was a bleak grey that mirrored a lifeless dawn sky exactly. There was no wind, no sunrise, and the whole presented a very drab picture. Then it happened. A big roach rolled. I think its head, or at least its head and shoulders came out first. I am sure, or at least I think its tail fin was the last thing to be seen. There was no noise and the whole movement created hardly any ripple. In fact the only dramatic things were the fleeting yet obvious signs that it had been a big fish and a

very momentary stab of colour. The silver of the scales had in that instant outshone the hoar frost – but especially it is that pulsing of red fins that sticks with me. That jab of crimson suddenly lit up the entire winter scene.

After that I often saw big roach roll, both at dusk and dawn. It was nearly always a sign that they were willing to feed and I often caught a fish after seeing it move on the top. Generally one, or perhaps two, roach moved but knowing that the shoals were so small I was in no way discouraged. Only twice did something quite out of the ordinary happen.

The first occasion took place one December day around mid-day. The weather was typical non-roach stuff, very clear and bright, coldly sunny with a stiff breeze. The river was crystal clear and I felt that I was a fool to be on the river at all during daylight and that I would have been better indoors until dusk and the first darkness hours.

I had had no bites and was walking the river to keep warm and keep up my interest when I got to the place I called Houseago Corner – after a close friend of those days. Right before me a roach rolled, a big one, and I sat down in stunned bewilderment. During the next hour on that bend I counted no less than 36 sightings: some were very probably made by the same fish, but still I reckoned on having seen at least nine different fish. They were very close to me, they were all very large, some were massive and over 3lb. For a while I wondered if they were in distress of some sort but then I noticed a heavy fly hatch on the bankside which the breeze was blowing onto the river. The roach were behaving exactly like trout on an evening rise and taking the struggling insects. I did not go down the bank for my tackle and anyway, I had no fly gear with me, so I merely sat and watched. I am glad now that I did for I have never seen such a sight before or since and I confess that I would not believe such a tale unless I had in truth seen it.

The second time was the following February when a harsh freeze-up was preceded, or perhaps blown in by, cruel east winds carrying icy droplets of rain on them that pecked the backs of a man's hands like angry chickens. I had thrown some mashed bread into the swim whilst I put up my rod and then shuffled into the swim tight under an alder bush. Right upstream into my face the wind was coming, raising tears in

my eyes, and pushing a few bits of floating crust into a slack at
my feet. The crusts were being lashed up against the reed bed
but, even as the rain came on heavier, a roach began to swirl at
them and actually took pieces down. I fished the slack very
carefully right into darkness without a bite of course.

Neither incident is typical but both do show that even a fish
can be as capricious as any other being on earth. Watching
such few fish as these in often heavy winter waters was
difficult, time consuming and not always rewarding. At times
I was forced to make guesses on the evidence I picked up. On
such clues, I felt then that big roach like these do not live in
swims, but merely use them for a while before passing onto
the next stop-over. There seems to be no pattern for their
movements and their progress up and down a mile or so of
river appears to have been very haphazard. During a one week
period I took a big roach twice in two nights on one swim and
then had him a third time four nights later half a mile upstream.

Probably big roach live in a swim whilst food remains there
or until they are disturbed away from it, perhaps by a pike or

by a cormorant, an otter or a human. A feeling tells me that it is possible that the appearance of a bream shoal can force roach out of an area – but I have no definite proof of this. Pike are so basic to the river's environment that their harassment of the roach cannot be grudged: neither can an otter's. They are fascinating vivacious animals whose right to live can never be denied. Cormorants though, are unlovely birds. To see them croaking in on an unfriendly wind bodes no good for an inland fishery with thin fish stocks and I will discourage them quite literally in any way I can.

Over the years I found a definite unpredictability in the swims that these big roach would favour. In general terms, they appeared to like deeper water, not still, but out of the main current, which had a harder bottom of gravel, sand or chalk, which had a depression or trough set into the bed to give a variety of depth and which had some sort of tree cover overhead. Having said all this, there was one swim that conformed perfectly with all these demands and yet I never once knew fish to stay in it. It was possible to climb the overhanging alders and see groups of roach travel through, completely ignoring food lying in the swim.

Still all my favourite ambush places, the places that I could expect travellers to drop off into, conformed in most respects and I have never found a good roach swim that has none of the guiding characteristics.

I would like to generalize and say that these big roach did not feed during daylight – but they did and not only if the river was running coloured. However, daylight feeding was the exception and was generally triggered off by some particular event – perhaps a sudden clouding of a previously bright sky, or by an influx of food, perhaps maggots or as on the day of the fly hatch, a natural bonanza. No, in nearly all cases the fish began to feed as dusk began to come in. Then they would become more active, rolling and splashing a few minutes before settling to feed.

Once started, they were likely to feed intermittently for anything between two and five hours – a period that could take them on close to midnight. If the night settled clear with a big moon and a quick frost, the spell of feeding could be long delayed, perhaps until three or four hours after sundown – but if roach were in the swim and had not been alarmed, then they were likely to eat eventually.

Dawn nearly always proved to be as active a period as dusk, again with a spell of rolling near first light and a steady feeding spell into the morning. Colder frosty dawns slowed the fish down considerably but a mist, drizzle or low cloud and rain proved ideal feeding conditions that would encourage them to be active well into the late morning.

As I said to Chris, I no longer know if big roach are present, for certainly after 1976–77 the population began to decline very obviously. They were, after all, very old fish and I do not think that any other explanation is needed but natural causes. From 1974, it had also been clear that these big roach were not spawning successfully. This, I believe, is the case with the large, old specimens of every species, and the roach were either not building up spawn or were failing to shed it properly. I wrote at the time of the decline that 'perhaps it is all part of a long term regenerative process that nature undertakes periodically. There have been roach in the Wensum since time immemorial, I cannot believe we should be so unlucky to see the last of them'.

At that time, I did think I was whistling rather in the dark and that such a long term cyclical process was unlikely. However, this summer, 1983, I met a team of Water Authority bailiffs and Fishery Scientists conducting a survey on the stretch in question. Certainly they confirmed that the river is no less pure, no less rich in food stocks, no less deep or quick flowing. There is not one real biological answer as to why the roach should be in decline.

I have also discovered a book published in the late 1930s which laments the disappearance of the once great roach shoals in the same river and doubts if they would ever return. They had returned by the mid 1950s at the latest and the fishing was splendid throughout the 1960s, tailing off in the disease year to produce the few large specimens I found myself with.

At this moment, there are pockets of young, healthy roach on the upper river and they back up my genuine belief that the river is undergoing one of its long periodic cycles. There is no proof of this, but it seems possible that a sequence of events could trigger the present stocks of roach to spawn widely and successfully in the next decade. The river would again become prolific until disease or disaster move in, kill the majority, produce a minority of huge fish once more and so complete the cycle.

JOHN NUNN'S ROACH

On Friday 6 January, just as I was leaving the house, John Nunn caught me on the phone. Big things were happening on the river. Could I get down to him? Had I got films in? Would I bring the flashgun? Like the days of old, the adrenalin ran freely, I drove madly, always excited at the thought of seeing a big fish. I pulled by his car, put on my Barbour and looked about me. A strong wind was piling up rain from the South, you could smell it was on its way. The flood plain looked barren, black and cold. I pulled up the hood and set off over the stile, walking very quickly upstream.

He was on the long straight, pacing round and round his umbrella, in a devastation of clinging mud and topsy turvy tackle. His hair was sodden, plastered over his face, the face of one of the most joyful anglers that I have seen anywhere. 'Well,' I said, 'where is it? What is it, for God's sake?'

'I'll tell you,' he replied. 'I came up here on a hunch. I thought I might as well blank here as anywhere else. I could hardly keep the rod on its rests with the wind and I was on the point of packing up when the bobbin just hit the butt. I was sure it was the wind, but I struck anyway in case. Right at the back of the strike, there was a clunk and something there.

I had to reel in fast to keep contact with him. The way the rod was juddering, I knew it had to be a big fish. The gusts of wind were a nightmare, pulling and pushing the rod, playing those screeching notes on the tight line. I knew if the fish wasn't firmly hooked, I could lose him especially when he swirled in the waves. It was so dark, I had to have the torch in my teeth when it came to net him, and the steep bank made the job even harder. He came into the beam, John, on his side, beaten and I saw for the first time that he was a roach, the biggest roach I'd ever dreamed of seeing.'

I set up the tripod, warmed the flashgun, set the camera exposures, measured distances out and cursed him for not letting me see the fish. He drew it from the sack and the next day, I printed photographs of a 3lb 3oz roach.

A man can fish his lifetime out without seeing a roach a third of that size. He will not be an unlucky man either, for there are areas of the country where a fish like John's would be quite beyond belief. You will not be surprised to know that John, myself and Roger Miller have fished that swim from that night to this. I had finished the roach chapter, but the spell reminded me of things forgotten . . . and taught me things anew.

Significantly, the area we are fishing is above one of the mills where the depth and width has more than doubled the average upstream and the speed of the current has consequently slowed considerably. So often, I have found that these stretches are the concentration points for the biggest roach from late autumn until March when they are most in need of shelter from cold and flood. There are no precise swims or holding areas on the big sheet of water we are fishing: we had looked in vain for conspicuous saucers in the bed, or any obstruction to slow the current down still more, but have found none. As a result, the fish tend to graze slowly up and down the whole quarter of a mile beat.

First Roger, fishing upstream, begins to get flickering bites as cautious roach move into his swim and then he hooks and lands one or two fish. All goes quiet and then my rod tip begins to move each cast and for fifteen minutes the shoal is with me. A cast comes and goes without a bite. I have lost them and John is next down the line for the action and after him, the roach will continue off downstream away from us, or come back past me and then Roger. The fish act much as a flock of sheep does, gradually covering a field.

The month has been a period of climatic extremes. Gales, heavy snow falls and then heavy rain onto a thaw produced floods. Nights of clear weather followed, hitting the river with often severe frosts, but despite all this, the roach have fed on and hardly a session has turned out to be biteless. It seems to bear out that if you can find river roach, then whatever the weather, the chances of catching a fish sometime are very high. At some point during the twenty-four hour cycle, they are going to feed.

In fact, the nights of frost have seemed to be the best. My

old beliefs that the warm clouded periods produced the longest feeding spells have been shattered. With fish, you can never say that you know, you can only guess. Big fish like these are in the end unknowable.

One of my best roach came on the coldest of nights. Before sundown, temperatures had hit zero, and, unhindered by the light wind, a freezing mist spread itself over the valley. It could not cloak the moon though, that rose nearly full and laid a silver veil wherever the fogs let it. The cold got deep inside me, a gnawing, numbing cold, the type that tires you, and saps any desire to re-cast or even tackle down and leave. The line had long since glued itself to the rod rings, and I noticed this but could not bother myself to try to thaw it out. Why should I? What roach would feed on a night like this with the river running brown, fast and margin frozen?

But a roach did take my bait, so well that though the line could not run, it pulled down the rod tip and was already well hooked by the time that I had moved.

The floods continue and all the way down the river, the mill gates are flung open. A month after John's fish was caught, nowhere on the non tidal river is fishable. Mud banks everywhere are visible and a channel of peat brown water races thin and shallow between them. After being so thrilled at the river's apparent recovery, I am suddenly so alarmed at the turn of the tide. What is happening to those slab sided, slow moving fish that spend their lives seeking cover and still water? How can they survive anywhere in this maelstrom unleashed upon them? Whilst the mills are owned by private individuals, who throw open their sluices at the first sign of rain, can there ever be a hope of any real roach revival in our river?

10 · *Rudd*

In our second season at Felbrigg, long before the place became famous, Sharon and I camped by the lake, in a clearing in Roundwood, at a point where the chimneys of the Hall look over the brow of the downs. We stayed there for three weeks and into a fourth dominated by a summer anti-cyclone that was pushing up from the Azores, bringing with it temperatures into the upper seventies and beyond.

Felbrigg was all but unknown. There were no tracks around the bank and we had to make them as we went. There were no swims cut either and we had to hack them out of the long grasses and field flowers. Only a handful of local anglers fished the lake and there were no lakeside walkers at that time. In fact, in all that period on the water we only saw one other human being.

FELBRIGG HALL.

That was Tom, the keeper. As good and as kind a man as you could hope to find. He was one of the old breed of keepers, a man who worked hard to raise his own birds rather than buy in weak flying fledglings. He rarely used a pub, other than to see who was about at closing time. He kept clear of cronies, though he would do anything for anyone. He knew how many birds to put down in the carr, how many up on the hill and how many to leave out of the wood. He knew the pests necessary to rid the estate of, and those that he could safely leave. He kept his cottage painted from window sill to gate and grew vegetables enough in the garden to keep him near enough the year round. He was tidy in his habits, made his last visits between ten and midnight and was round again at five to check against the 'first lighter'.

And so he woke me one morning. Sharon had been fishing since three, but I had fallen into one of those lapses that overtake all long vigil fishermen from time to time. When extreme tiredness sets in, all one can do is relax and give in to it, for otherwise consequences can be dangerous. I was in a deep sleep when the blast came. All I knew was that the world had come to an end. My blurred eyes saw a spinning blue sky and patches of canvas green. I heard pheasants and jays and thunder rolled into one. But as life steadied around me there was Tom, breaking the gun above me, shifting a cartridge and laughing till the tears appeared.

He never minded us being there and in part I suppose we represented company in that quiet place. We probably discouraged poachers as well and in part our presence helped to get rid of the big flocks of Canada Geese that he hated so much. They mucked up the meadow no end and muddied up the gin clear water of the lake down one bank. They chased a lot of duck away from the shallows and rooted up the weed there as well. The food stocks in the weed were spoilt, as were the spawning grounds of the tench. Some eggs might have been lost, and certainly there was less shelter for the fry. Altogether, he thought them noisy good for nothing birds and when they left in our second week he gave us part of the credit.

Tom's dog, Jester, I think was more the cause, chasing them at least twice a day and then stopping on the meadow to dig up a mole or two. He was a good labrador with a nose for anything amiss. Once he even went into the water for my rod lost to the run of a wild tench while I was cooking breakfast. He retrieved it neatly, butt in mouth, and the tench was still there to be landed.

Tom and Jester were both important to the place, but it was the quality of the rudd that made it seem nigh on perfect. It is quite possible to catch small beautiful rudd and there are waters where the species grows large but begins to lose that freshness, the sparkle and the gleam of the unmarked, untouched fish. Here in 1974, the rudd were very large and wonderful to look at. They had the small heads and massive shouldered backs of true big fish whilst their scales kept the true golden yellow and unspoilt patterns of small fish. Their fins were an indescribable tangerine orange merging into flame red at the tips. Chris Turnbull's drawing of the leaping rudd is above my desk now and looking at it, I could feel that it is too perfect, too idealized a vision of the species, had I not known Felbrigg rudd in those days.

In fact, this has always been one of the real purposes of my fishing. So many times have I just wanted to see the fish, to hold it for a second, to be able to drink in every detail and for a fraction of time to have it in my world. The excitement of the bite, the thrill of the battle, the pride in its weight are all part of the picture but they do not compare to that fleeting unforgettable moment when the creature that has always been just a glimpse far out in the water, is actually in your grasp. That these rudd were so heavenly perfect was the last bit of the jigsaw that made Felbrigg edenic.

I wanted to pitch a swim from the dam wall, from which I could cast 30–40yds into the deepest water of the lake and to do that a lot of weed would need to be moved. So, at the start of a hot still day I paddled the dinghy from the boat house and began to drag a channel through starwort, water buttercup even and milfoil. I worked for seven hours, sometimes swimming in the cool clear water when the day became intolerably hot, and by evening I had unloaded over 20 hold fulls of the stuff.

I mention this to show how neglected the place was but above all, because in all my weed cutting years only twice before have I found plants so rich in crustaceans, insects and molluscs. In patches, the weeds on the rowing boards heaved with lice, shrimps, crickets, pondskaters, beetles, water scorpions, boatmen, the nymphs of damsel and dragon and alder flies, the larvae of mosquitoes and phantom midges, eared pond snails, ramshorn snails, marsh snails and mussels. In the bright sunlight and the baking heat, those that could fled the cut dying weed following rivulets of water to get back to safety and cool darkness. For minutes at a time I merely sat watching this sad exodus knowing how difficult it would be for two anglers on their own, with obviously limited supplies of artificial bait, ever to wean the rudd off this abundant natural larder onto foods strange to them.

In fact, such was the case for in those early days at Felbrigg the rudd were much more difficult to catch than they later became when maggots started to be introduced in very large quantities. Indeed, the really massive catches came in March, when the lake life was running low and anglers' maggots probably provided the biggest food source. This is not an uncommon problem in rich, underfished waters where the stocks of fish are low and until the lake receives heavier attention from anglers or until there is a cold, wet poor weed summer catches are meagre.

Elsewhere on the lake, there are few areas to fish from other than tiny clearings in which to place baits before individual rudd, but the points to watch them from were numerous. All along one bank were tall trees and at twenty feet up there was a clear view across yards of water. One fallen tree – an elm I suppose – led us thirty feet out into the lake itself and I built a kind of nest at the end where I could sit and watch, hidden by dead branches, for hours. There was a small marshy island in the shallows at the Northern end of the lake and I laid planks to it through the mire. Rudd used the area extensively by the early mid afternoon, appearing an arms length from me and drifting past lazily untroubled, unsuspecting. There was even the boat I could float in, brushed over the water by the wind, lying in the gunwales, just a head over the side, polaroid glasses on, seeing through weed to the fish moving past.

The pattern of those twenty odd days remained largely the same. We fished hard from the hour before dawn, say about 3am until around 6. At some point fish were quite likely to pass down the dam channel and a rudd – but never more than two – was always a possibility.

Between 6 and 9am, the fish seemed to move away from the dam and I began to stalk the shoals as they moved up the tree lined bank. It was not light enough in the sky and water to see them, yet not too bright to stop them from feeding.

Breakfast at around nine was always an event, treasured as a change from the water, the concentration and the rudd. It was good mentally, to switch off and relax for an hour, talking about anything other than fish or fishing. The curl of smoke above the trees often brought Jester down the walk from the cottage. First we would hear the pheasants scampering in the runs, then the bracken breaking back and then his bright button face and wet nose would be there hovering over the pan.

From 10 until 4pm the time passed watching from the trees, the island or the boat, sometimes dozing in the sun, but hardly ever fishing. There would have been no point to it. The rudd just did not feed on those bright hot days. Indeed from 4 until

7pm, they seemed to disappear altogether, ghosting into the thickest weed beds with only the slightest movements to indicate their presence there. This was the time we chose to sleep. It was quite cool in the wood and the tent kept out a lot of the light, but the flies were always bad, scratching on the canvas and running along your lips as you tried to forget them.

Jester often woke us up around seven, rummaging outside among the fallen branches, nosing at the ties to the flap and barking in his short sharp yelps. He knew it was time for our second meal of the day and over it we might talk to Tom as we ate and prepared our gear for the night session. He never stayed long, because the midges got to him and he and Jester went off back into the wood; after five minutes there would be a chink of light from his sitting room.

Fishing began at eight o'clock. Serious fishing this, during the time that the rudd were the most likely to feed. The Park became very quiet with just the sounds of far away cars on the coast road and in the wood the owls and stoats and creatures of the night beginning to stir. Almost all of those nights were cloudless and well lit enough to see duck coming in to the top shallows and on occasion a rudd shoal working along the weed beds towards our prebaited channel. If they stopped there the fishing could be fast until around 1.00am when the lake began to grow still. Most nights, therefore, there was time for a couple of hours in the tent, sleeping, again before the next day's cycle began.

The rudd in Felbrigg were true shoal fish. From the evidence we saw the lake's entire rudd population was divided into three groups of fish. One small shoal of around a dozen fish were quite huge rudd. I put baits to these fish frequently but they never showed interest. Almost certainly they must have come into my channel at sometime but I never landed one, so I am unsure about their exact weight. Most, I am sure, were, however, over 3lb and perhaps the largest two or three fish were nearer four. The two other groups of rudd were much more numerous and I did take fish from them, all between 1½lb and just under 3lb.

These rudd did not, like a lot of lake fish, simply gather to exploit favourable situations at particular times. Nor like dace or river roach had they simply found a small swim favourably

placed amongst the currents; but rather they spent the entire time together as a group. They never separated, even in the drifting lazy periods they hung close. Generally though they faced all points of the compass when they rested in a hole in the weed. This could have been mere chance or a haphazard grouping but more probably, as a shoal, they were always alive to danger. This way they were highly tuned to disturbance from the bank, from the air and from the water and weed jungle itself. If one fish moved in alarm, so did the others in complete synchronization.

In a way, they were mirrored by the flock of Canada Geese. Whenever the birds grazed, a look-out remained vigilant on one of the hillocks. The post was rotated, each bird taking ten or so minutes on watch. This way a stray walker, or farm labourer was quickly noticed and the flock would be warned onto the water.

The shoals operated on a very precise time clock with predictable patrol patterns around the lake. Without definite proof of this, the dominant force that summer seemed to be the following of the sun. For example, by six o'clock the sun's rays were striking the western tree lined bank and that is where they first appeared, moving from the deeper dam wall into the warming shallows. A very cool night and thick mist on the water kept them deeper for longer and they might not then move until breakfast time.

Generally, by the early afternoon two or even all three of the shoals would be laying up in the weeded, reeded shallows at the northern end, around the island. The fish appeared to love the sun warmed water, especially the areas where the scum and debris of the air had fallen and where no breeze ruffled the surface. The water was as warm as milk and the fish frequently rolled right over in it, their brassy sides flashing as they caught the sunlight. Only in the mid, late afternoon did the heat seem to become too extreme and if there were no breeze then they moved into the weed beds themselves, sometimes tenting it upwards, occasionally waving out a red fin. Once more they were in tune with the geese which dozed on the pasture and the cattle that sheltered against the hedgerow.

Around eight, when the sun had sunk behind the wood, they became more active, gradually leaving the shallows and moving off into the deeper body of the lake. Obviously we could not see them closely any more, but at times we heard them roll, saw vague disturbances, and at times caught them out there. If there were to be a general feeding period we always expected it at last light or those two hours into darkness.

These movements were only followed and were at all predictable whilst the heat wave lasted. It was broken twice during the period, each time by nearly twenty four hours of blustery winds and rapidly falling temperatures. On each occasion, as far as I could see, fish kept away from the shallows, keeping farther out in the deeper water. Now, they fed much more readily. During the hot settled spells feeding had been erratic and it seemed as if the rudd could go for days without any noticeable food intake whatever. Once the weather changed to break this fact they were ravenous. Still dusk proved to be the strongest feeding period, but now fish could be guaranteed, fishing into the face of the wind with a thick cloud cover overhead. The rudd were obviously moving more, eager, positively looking for food. Bites became unmissable rather than the tentative twitches of previous nights. Several fish could be taken from the shoal before it became so scared that it moved away. The shoals stayed in the channel, feeding well past midnight and once I took fish periodically through till dawn.

The rudd rolled close in on these dark windy nights. As with all fish, the movement is a sign of feeding activity and the harder they rolled, the more would be caught from the channel that night. They came out head first, you would see them as dark shapes poised over the steel grey ripples for a second, stood on their tail and then falling back with a distinctive crash, more noisy than the movement of a tench three times their size. All the lethargy of the previous days had gone within hours, replaced with a vibrant energy and a desire for food so great that fishing two rods was frequently impossible.

Felbrigg nine years on still produces good rudd and always will unless total pollution strikes. The strain of the fish is perfect, and I have already said how rich the lake is in food supplies. Indeed some nights so dense was the mosquitoe hatch and so thick lay the sticky pupae cases that they clogged the lines making it quite impossible to continue with fishing at all. The rising insects hung like mist over the water until the far bank was all but veiled by them.

But, by the late 1970s, many of the very big fish had gone. Age must have accounted for several as must increased fishing pressure, bad handling and retention in keepnets injured others. Probably more vital is the fact that in the mid 1970s the lake was eel netted. The removal of this important predator led to an explosion of the lake's tench population which had been previously kept under control. Now there could take place a reversal of the role domination in the water with the rudd taking second best to the stronger tench.

At the same time, the once prolific perch stocks were hit, probably by disease, and the numbers of small rudd surviving increased dramatically. Those three original shoals of big rudd now found themselves in a busy tench water surrounded by large numbers of small fish and their progress suffered.

Such is the fragility of an inland species. Felbrigg at its peak was perfect for this study: big fish, clear water, undisturbed banks and environment and I like to think I made the most of it in the days of Tom and Jester.

11 · *Tench*

A SPECIAL TENCH

The path led through a wood and alongside a lake. There was a commotion in amongst the trees and I am almost sure it was jays squabbling – though it is over twenty years since that day dawned and I could be imagining details that did not exist. But I can still see the gate at the end of the trackway, remember climbing over it and approaching a man fishing beneath a chestnut tree.

It was mid-morning and the sun was well up, flooding through the water, picking out weed fronds, swan mussels, shoals of roach and perch, but the man pointed my gaze down deeper into the swim before us. Two slow moving shadows were grazing over a bed of mashed bread and he whispered 'tench, great old tench' and I was spellbound. So in that summer, and summers 1959, 1960 and 1961 I climbed over that gate many times when the mist was rising off the lake and the meadows, but I never hooked a single tench and got so that I never even expected to. But the law of averages tilted my way and at last in 1962, in July, I hooked, played and landed my first tench.

It was, of course, a special tench because it was my first, but also because I came to know a lot about that individual fish. She and I had lives that came together again in the future. Much later I wrote a favourite piece about her:

It was very late evening in the waning summer. The islands out in the lake were dark, like monsters, and the boy could distinguish nothing further than the end of the dam sluices. He never saw his float dip, the rod just pulled down in his hands.

He could hardly see his first tench either, when it lay on the stone dam, but with his fingers he felt the smoothness of its skin and the power of its short stumpy body. He swung his small keep net out into the black water and tied it to the iron grill of the old eel trap. As the fish slid through his hands into the throat of the net he realised it was only a small tench – but his first! He knew he must show someone, prove his skill, and as he ran home through the forest he knew that the dusty days had been all worthwhile. Back at the lake night sank in behind him. Deer came down to drink, witch black herons flew in over the trees to roost, only the small tench was caged, bulldozing against the meshes of the net.

Early the next morning the boy and his mother came down the track. They saw the water shine and the sluices bright in the sunlight and a heron standing over the net. The boy ran round the head of the lake and the heron rose up and away over the islands. Small and dark the tench floated in the net, so they lifted it out and the boy cried a while. Two dark red holes through its back, just under the dorsal fin showed clearly, but tench are strong and the woman noticed that the little red eye still moved and the gills still worked, so she held it steady in the water and waited. For over an hour they watched the fish struggle and then its tail fin began to beat and gently it moved away growing darker and darker until they could only see a thin line of bubbles arrowing out to the islands. During Christmas 1962 the first cold winds from the North East began to blow and the ten weeks of hard frosts had started. By early January the swans on the lake were dying and, as the water iced thicker, bittern perished in the reed beds. In the February evenings the estate workers skated on the lake and made bonfires on the shore against the arctic winds that crackled through the frozen forests. Beneath the skates the bream were beginning to die – nights and days circling up through the water nearer the ice-cap searching for the dis-appearing oxygen. But the tench with the twin scars pulled herself deeper into the mud with her great pectoral fin and slept through the blizzards. She slept through the night in March when the ice sheet finally overwhelmed the dam wall and burst through it, slithering away into the new plantation behind the lake. By morning, water rats had gathered there and were feeding ravenously on the pale bream – some had found the ice-encrusted body of the wicked heron.

When the slow spring finally came and the tench at last pushed clear from the bottom ooze, she found the lake a new, strange place. It was quiet without the vast wandering hordes of bream and the thick shoals of roach. The groups of tench found the feeding richer now they were almost sole possessors of all the water.

Through the next years of hot summers the scarred female tench grew fast. Her body lost the shades of olive and brown, and deepened to black. Her fins thickened into paddles as large as the palm of a man's hand and during the early summers when she was round with spawn she was near ten pounds in weight. She was a changed fish from the 'baby' caught seven years before – only the scars remained on her flanks – and in her mind. She avoided the dam wall now and always would, and she never looked at anglers' baits again, but drank in the daphnia filled water, or sucked the writhing bloodworms from the silt beds. That day had taught her a strange wisdom.

In the year 1969 many miles away up the valley a tired farm labourer was backing his tractor into the shed for the night. Over the din of the engine he didn't hear the thud as he hit the stack of pesticide drums: in the dusk, he didn't see one roll down the slope into the stream. By dawn it was filtering into the lake.

First the algae and daphnia began to fade until the water turned crystal clear. Then the mussels opened and rotted: the last carp in the western bay washed into the weed fringe: the small male tench began to litter the windward shore. But the scarred tench and a knot of companions went to the deep gorge between the islands where the water was fresh. Then it too grew foul. On the fourth night a male fish accompanying her began to tremble and float up through the polluted layers of water. So she left the deeps and moved slowly up the dying lake. By the early summer dawn she had found the feeder stream, running clear again. That was when the man saw her again, resting in the sunlight of the new day, and he hardly believed her size.

For over two years he fished the lake in pursuit of her. Apart from the eels that made their way in from the sea and the near-by salt marshes, the great tench was the only fish left in the lake. His time was without reward, apart from the beauty of the lonely dawns and the still warm nights he loved so much. Twice he saw her: once in the north shallows, cruising down past the pine trees as evening drew in. One dawn her back humped through the misty water before him and he had the vision of a great sweep of tail and knew she was still alive.

On one day in summer 1972 a man brought a boat down through the forest and spread his eel nets across the lake. Then he returned to his caravan to wait a night and day before pulling them in again. Next day he went out for a meal and fell in with some old friends. He had too much to drink, fell ill and lay all alone for two days, forgetting all about his nets.

As the netter slept in his nightmares, the tench entered the trap. She cut her fins trying to escape and bruised her lips on the meshes. The sun rose high and drained the shallows of oxygen so her gills had to pump quickly to breathe at all. And the frightened eels chased to bite her as they hurried past down the corridors of net. Bit by bit the life of the old fish drained away.

The shape hanging in the nets just beneath the surface worried the lone angler, worried him so much that he went to his van for his binoculars. Through them the tench was clear. He ran up the bank to the boathouse and pulled at the lock. It fell away, rotten like the punt inside. So he took his knife and strapped it round his waist, kicked off his boots and swam out to the long nets. Treading water, he hacked at the twine and ripped the meshes off the fish. Cradling her in his arms he waded off to the island and sat in the cool water. The big black body swayed in his hands and the fins began to stir the water. He remembered a morning ten years before – and knew she would live!

I did feel very close to that fish and at the time, I was proud of the story I wrote on her. Now, I wonder if I exaggerated my own part in it, but even so, I still feel that the tale has validity, if only to show the possible dangers that any big fish is likely to face. No modern inland water anywhere in Europe can expect to escape all disasters for the lifespan of a tench, a carp or a bream. Twenty, thirty, or even forty years represents a very long time in what have become vulnerable environments.

Tench fishing should always be about happy times and every tench fisher has happy tales to tell. Very many of mine come from the King's Water on the East Coast and I owe my knowledge of it to John Nunn, the man who I suppose is my oldest fishing partner. The King's Water, named so as it was dug in the time of Charles II to hide up his fleet from the raiding Dutch. When the foreigners had sailed up the estuary, past the mouth of the water, the English ships could emerge and the ambush could be well and truly sprung. I don't doubt the truth of the story, after all it is easy now to dredge up the stems and bowls of clay pipes which in such numbers must have belonged to a navy of ancient mariners.

My first evening there was damp and dreary with a sea fret that struck cold and put the tench so much off their feed, that neither of us had had a bite by dark. We rowed back to the staging and prepared for a night in the old railway waggon, a nest of a place that I would get to know well in the years following. The hissing tilly threw its flickering light over this

wooden palace, over the nets, the oars, the weighing scales, an armoury of ready made up rods and our two sleeping bags.

A cup of soup each and a half bottle of port and still an hour before sleep so we talked fishing stories. Huge fish we knew of ourselves or by hearsay; fish that got away and yet to come. We slid back the door on its stout runners and heard the foghorn moan and the peewits scream on the lonely marsh. Some came close and the lantern reflected on their snow white chests and then the moist air came in and we settled back. I told the tale of the huge catfish, exactly as it had been told me. How a friend had been exploring a secret estate lake, reputed by legend almost to hold these special fish, and how for hours he had seen nothing, and then in the clear shadows, a form of strange shape but huge size came gliding past him to disappear into the gloom of a central channel. It seemed an eery tale for a benighted spot such as this one, and we settled in then and there and the alarm clock was the only sound other than our breathing and the occasional whisper of wind through cracks in the panels.

We woke at the beginning of a perfect dawn, still and bright

with a five o'clock sun drawing up the dew and making the world warm by six. It brought the tench on to feed in exactly the way all the text books since Walton have said they should. The clusters of bubbles blossomed gold in the slanting sun's rays which also laid a blue sheen of light across the oily surface of our two swims. The tench rolled often, rollicking on the surface, splashing the floats in quick black silhouettes against the bright eastern light. Bites too came as they should, dithering the float until I or John went too crazy to hold back a strike and when they were on, they fought hard and deep in water clear enough to see them running.

Trip after trip to the King's Water was good like this: I have never driven off the marsh there without feeling the deep satisfaction of a successful fisherman and the only fault of the place is to have made me lazy. If on other waters I have not caught tench I have never analysed why and never made any real attempt to get into their world. Fortunately, friends of mine have.

TENCH OF PIT AND LAKE

Chris Turnbull has fished extensively for tench in the larger gravel pits whilst Martyn Page knows as well as anyone the tench type of the larger, shallower lakes.

We all three work in the city centre and there is the inevitable bar equidistant from each of us so that lunchtimes have taken on a new and fish directed aspect for us. In the depths of winter with falling leaves and rain outside, it is good to be sitting with friends talking about tench and thinking of summer when all around you there are worried city faces.

Repeatedly, I have stressed the impossibility of generalisation and the point has been made that different fish of the same species behave uniquely, according to the environment. It is probable that of all our freshwater fish, this is truest with tench for the gravel pit tench that Chris knows could nearly be a different species from Martyn's tench of the small, silting estate lake.

Both waters are very rich in natural foods however, and in neither place are the stocks of tench large. Also, in both waters the tench are the dominant species, not challenging for their

existence with bream, or more particularly with carp. This freedom from want and competition allows them to develop their natural characteristics without becoming involved in a struggle for mere survival. Because of all these factors, the fish grow large in both the pit and the lake and they represent perfect examples for study.

A lunch session discussing tench with Martyn and Chris has to be lively: they know their water and their fish and they have seen different things. The tench themselves are in many ways quite dissimilar. The pit tench tend to be long for their weight. They are muscular and fight hard, long and fast. In fact, they have adapted to a large environment which they use extensively. Chris has on occasions followed fish around the entire perimeter of the fifty acre water, watching them swim continuously at a speed a little less than walking pace.

Pit fish have well established patrol routes that take them along bars, following weed beds and wind changes that rarely allow them long periods of inactivity. A comparison can be made with pike: loch pike tend to be long, lean and hard fighting because they too inhabit large waters and are highly mobile following shoals of quick moving salmon or seatrout.

The lake fish that Martyn knows are less nomadic tench: their water has less dramatic depth changes, it is smaller and the tench make much less positive movement. In general, these fish tend to drift where the winds and underwater currents take them, move more slowly and with less immediate purpose. This more lethargic life style has meant that the tench are shorter, plumper and fight less well. They do not move as quickly through the water and tire much more easily.

Both Martyn and Chris are agreed that tench become very easily occupied, in fact the most quickly so of all fish, but even this basic trait manifests itself differently. In the lake, the tench are very quick to go off artificial, angler introduced foods like maggots, casters and corn, and are very quick to go back on to natural food only. Probably, the population levels are the key to this situation, in so far as the fish numbers are so low that there are always quite adequate natural food supplies. The fish do not need to take the hooking risk to stay well fed.

There is on the lake a strange, as yet unexplained, phenomenon. The tench there will quickly take the free offerings of particle baits such as peas and maples when they are newly introduced. If caught, they will re-gurgitate large quantities of these new foods, but they will not take any samples of the new baits on a hook for at least until the next season. The only feasible answer to this behaviour is that the terminal rig frightens them, yet with the use of the most modern hair and bolt rigs, this almost certainly is not the case. When Martyn told Chris and myself this tale neither of us could think of an answer to it. Looking at the dregs in the glasses, we agreed that the tench can be the most inexplicable of fish. I realized too, that it was my round.

At the pit, according to Chris, the situation is very nearly exactly the reverse. There, any new food introduced will often be taken very quickly, even instantly, but its success as a bait is equally rapidly short-lived. If however, a new flavour or a new colour is added to the basic food then the interest of the tench will revive again for a while. Chris believes this to be the case because of the inquisitiveness of tench, because they are one of the most curious of fish. In the pit they have become quick to investigate bright food colours, reds, yellows and oranges, they are quick to home in onto splashes or colouring of the water, and they are keen to taste new flavours and smells. Martyn would agree to an extent to this in his lake fish – but it does seem likely that the more advanced baiting programmes on the pit have rendered the tench there more susceptible to the angler's artificials. Because the lake is left more alone, for longer periods of the tench season, the fish are naturally more aloof and less keen to change their feeding habits.

It seems, as if forever, tradition has had it that the peak tench feeding period is from dawn to sometime in the early/mid morning at which time the fish go into a kind of doze and lurk uncatchable until, perhaps, a short feeding period before dusk. Over the past years – say since the late 1970s – more advanced tench fishers have blown this concept sky high, and on both the pit and the lake it is realised that tench are quite likely to feed at any time during the twenty-four hours and that peak feeding periods can in fact alter through the years. Martyn pointed out that in the 1970s the lake did respond in those time honoured early morning spells and that fish had virtually

never been known to feed during the night. However, in the late 70s and early 1980s the tench changed their life patterns, beginning to feed at any time, quite haphazardly, and during 1983 the fish started to feed most reliably during the night itself, particularly between midnight and dawn, those very hours once considered to be the deadest of the angling clock.

Chris agrees and adds his experiences of the Pit tench where obviously similar things have happened to their behavioural patterns. There, four and five years ago, the tench fed hardest and most frequently during the daytime. Three years ago though, their spells became predominantly during the dawn and early morning period with a shorter burst at dusk. The next year the tench started to feed almost exclusively during the hours of darkness and the peak time emerged as 1am–2am – the hour most useless for most other species, the very doldrums of the night. Finally, in summer 1983, the cycle changed once more when the tench could come onto the feed at quite literally any hour of the twenty-four with no pattern at all appearing. My immediate response to this was that angling pressure and the catching and re-catching of individual fish was the only possible cause for this behaviour phenomenon. Neither Martyn nor Chris were at all impressed by this most direct of answers for, after all, Chris argued, on the pit anglers now fish round the clock for the tench, camping for a week or longer. The fish cannot possibly accept any time as a safe feeding period in these conditions. On the lake, Martyn added, angling pressure is so slight and so few fish are ever caught, that it seems unlikely that it is anglers alone that are remoulding these natural patterns. Much more likely, both feel, is the species itself reacting to complex as yet unknown environmental changes.

For a long time, most fishermen would agree that most species roll on the surface in some fashion before going down to feed. Bream, barbel, carp, rudd, roach – in fact nearly all freshwater fishes conform to this behaviour pattern. So it is with tench – a rolling tench is about to become a feeding tench – or so I thought. Chris suggests that even here tradition can be challenged. Perhaps with his artist's eye, or because of his experience of so many sessions on the pit, he feels that he had distinguished two totally different types of tench rolling behaviour.

The first rolling movement he recognizes is the gentle 'porpoising' action that is so familiar to all tench anglers. The head, shoulders, back, dorsal and then tip of the tail fin break the surface in that order in what is a virtually noiseless gliding movement – not unlike a trout feeding during a buzzer hatch. Chris feels from his experience that such a porpoising tench is a moving fish, a fish on its travels and not at all necessarily a fish preparing to feed. He has often watched tench moving in such a way travel for hundreds of yards, generally along gravel bars, without ever stopping to go down or feed at all. Sometimes the tench will make a dozen or more such appearances along its route.

The second tench roll that he has learnt to recognize is of a very different nature and purpose. This is how Chris describes the action:

A tench sees some food – or say an angler's bait in the clear water we get in the Pit, about two to four feet down – it stops and, very often, just like a carp, it will become curious and

start to circle the food area. It might go around the food area two, three or even four times before making a firm decision. If it is positive and decides to eat the food, it thrusts its shoulders down and flicks its tail up whereupon it appears very briefly on the surface in a splashy movement. The last thing you see on the bank is the tail waving vertically before going down over the food. In the porpoise movement, the tail is more parallel to the water, than vertically above it.

I think that this is worth a drink. Martyn agrees, though only to a point. He does believe that it is often better to have tench rolling in the swim next door than in yours itself, but still, generally if he sees tench rolling in the lake he believes that they are going to feed somewhere very quickly.

I am very keen to talk about the tench style of bubbling which again I have always thought of being one of the most common characteristics of the species. The idea of tench bubbles, though, quite obviously excites neither man not one jot. In the lake, Martyn says, it is very difficult indeed even to differentiate between fish bubbling and the bottom simply breathing in an undisturbed way. He has seen the tench bubble very infrequently at the lake in fact and he wonders if they actively dislike the bottom and if the two hundred year accumulation of silt and leaf mould proves too noxious for them to root in. In the pit, the look of a tench bubble depends on the type of ground that the fish is working over and the way the fish is attacking it in a search for food. A vigorous tench over a soft bottom obviously results in massive disturbance but a fish simply picking over gravel will produce nothing at all on the surface.

The only type of bubbles that Martyn is really happy fishing to is the *fizzy* type; an eruption of these tiny bubbles produces an almost frothy effect on the water surface. Eels, carp, and crucian carp all produce the fizzy bubbles when feeding hard and the tench is no exception.

We all agree that every freshwater species shoals, at least at certain times, but in the case of tench again, shoaling behaviour is not straightforward. Graham Marsden, the well known big fish hunter and writer, has suggested that rather than shoaling in the accepted sense, tench *families* would be a better description for their groupings. This theory fits in with Chris' experience on the pit where he feels the tench form small bands of three or four fish, of all sizes, which travel and feed together over a long period of time. Occasionally, large catches of tench are made on the pit when these families converge into one area for spawning, or because of certain weather conditions or because of some abnormally large or attractive food supply, but this is not usual. Much more common is for the angler to experience a handful of bites as the family appears, and land one or two fish before the scared, disrupted group moves off into the unfished water.

This kind of distinctive shoaling pattern is not Martyn's experience at the lake. There, he feels, the vast majority of the lake's population seem to hang together, very loosely, in the same general area of the water. It is not a tight grouping situation but a very disjointed, exploded shoaling habit. This conglomeration of tench keeps together as it uses different areas of the lake at different times, in different conditions. In periods of cold winds, the fish will drift *en masse* down towards the dam end of the lake where the water is deeper and warmer. Similarly when the temperatures begin to rise – or rather as barometer pressure begins to rise, they evacuate the dam area and slowly move back towards the previously over exposed shallows two hundred yards away. Of course, Martyn stresses, during the course of all these movements, the body of tench does subdivide to some extent but we are never looking at select individually motivated families in any way.

Over and over, we are examining the cycles of inland fisheries; the way weed, big fish and fish populations come and go in each water. Big perch for example have very short cycles whilst carp have, at the other extreme, exceptionally long cycles and a carp water can remain productive for decades. Whilst both the pit and the lake still have existing stocks of large tench both my drinking partners see problems for them in the near future. An analysis of these problems shows just how fragile inland fisheries can be.

On the pit an explosion of small roach will make the small food supplies of the water that the tench so depend upon less easy to come by. It is unlikely that angler introduced foods are going to make up the balance. Simple accident, to which

[131]

inland waters are so prone, has had its effect in the form of heavy rain, flooding, a breached bank and the loss of at least a proportion of the big tench. Nature being what it is, this might serve to help increase the food proportion available to the tench left . . .

The cycle of the lake is more obscure, has progressed further and the tench there are more dangerously in decline. In brief, in the 1960s the lake held very large stocks of rudd, roach, eels, perch, pike and tench but quickly all but the tench began to die away. These of course profited from the decrease of competition for food to become the large fish they are today.

'Ginger Beer', I thought whilst Martyn was talking through the lake's history, and my mind went back to a heatwave day in 1962 when I was abandoned for eleven hours on the water with cheese sandwiches and 'water, water everywhere and not a drop to drink'. The sight of my parents, the red brick country estate pub and a pint of ginger beer meant more than all of the hundred or so fish I had caught that day!

Those large tench survivors reached a peak between 1975 and 1977, whilst since a steady noticeable decline in their numbers has been accelerating. It is quite possible that today there are no more than twenty or thirty fish left in the lake and that they have only survived longer than the rudd or the roach or the perch because of their natural longevity.

No scientific research in the lake has been undertaken; any reasons for its decline must as yet remain entirely unproven, but the possibilities we three eagerly examine.

Bearing in mind the possible/probable complete demise of the lake's fish population, the possibility that the water itself is contaminated does exist. This does seem unlikely: there is no obvious seepage of chemical, sewerage or nitrate into the water: the lake is largely spring fed and the surrounding land is original pasture so that run off should not be a problem.

The other species died away before the existence of a problem was recognized – observing now the tench, the most serious question lies in their spawning habits. They are not reproducing successfully. Perhaps their age is telling against them. Perhaps the males have already nearly died out – most of the fish Martyn knows to have been caught are female. Weed samplings have produced none of the fingerling small fish that we would expect.

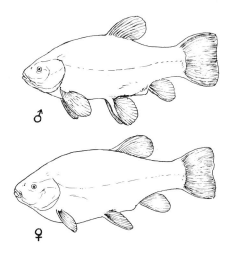

A third problem exists: the overwintering of cormorants upon the lake. The tench population is ailing, and these black, rapacious, flying birds could prove a further threat to young fish. They stop every winter on the lake for a while and we all suspect them of mopping up any smaller tench that could be forcing through. The birds obviously stay for something: the eel population is tiny, nothing else but tench exists in the lake, so into their craw might be going the future of the water.